Thomas Wood is a barrister specialising in employment law. He is known for his technical expertise and ability to tackle the most complex cases, working across a variety of sectors. He appears regularly before the employment tribunal in cases of wide variety.

Thomas has particular experience in discrimination claims where, throughout his career, he has been instructed to act and advise both for and against some of the largest organisations in the country, often in complicated or high-value claims.

# A Practical Guide to the Law in relation to Menopause and Perimenopause in the Workplace

# A Practical Guide to the Law in relation to Menopause and Perimenopause in the Workplace

Thomas Wood
Barrister, Gray's Inn
LLB (Hons) (Dunelm)

Law Brief Publishing

Published 2022 by Law Brief Publishing, an imprint of Law Brief Publishing Ltd
30 The Parks
Minehead
Somerset
TA24 8BT

www.lawbriefpublishing.com

Paperback: 978-1-914608-19-3

# PREFACE

There is currently no specific workplace protection for those experiencing menopause/perimenopause. However, it is a topic that is rising in prominence. That is because current employment law is deemed to be inadequate to protect those experiencing menopause/perimenopause. They are not protected any more than any other employee. There is no recognition that menopause/perimenopause is a protected characteristic, despite the difficulties it can cause. There is plenty of discussion around changing this.

In the meantime, however, those experiencing menopause and consequent disadvantages in the workplace, or even dismissal, must rely on the law as it presently stands. This book looks to outline that law, and set out where protection can be gained and where claims for compensation can arise.

When one considers where menopause/perimenopause fits within the current legislative scheme, the Equality Act 2010 immediately comes to mind. It is a period of life that affects women, and does so at a certain age. There is also the right not to be unfairly dismissed, which may be relevant depending on the particular effects of menopause / perimenopause. Those are the principal applicable areas. This book focuses on those areas and the potential claims within the employment tribunal jurisdiction. The text will pull together all the relevant law and will work through the legislation, codes of practice (mainly the Equality and Human Rights Commission Employment Statutory Code of Practice ('EHRC Code') and its supplement), and case law. It will look at the level of protection, and whether there are useful arguments that can be deployed to increase that. Overall, this book seeks to provide practitioners with a reference guide for dealing with a menopause-related employment tribunal claim.

Note that the law cited is accurate as at 31.03.2022.

Thomas Wood
April 2022

# CONTENTS

# CHAPTER ONE

# WHAT IS MENOPAUSE / PERIMENOPAUSE AND HOW DOES IT INTERACT WITH EMPLOYMENT LAW?

## What is menopause

Menopause is the time at which a woman stops having menstrual periods. It is marked by the last menstrual period, and is usually diagnosed after the passage of 12 months from that date. It is then dated retroactively.

Perimenopause (meaning 'around menopause') is the period of time beginning with irregular menstrual periods. This can be some years (between four and eight) before the last menstrual period and ending 12 months after it (i.e. the first 12 months of the post-menopause period). It is in that time that various physical changes take place. When most people talk about 'going through the menopause', they are in fact referring to perimenopause. However, for ease and consistency with general understanding, rather than differentiate between perimenopause and menopause, although they are distinct matters, this book will refer simply to menopause to cover the perimenopause period.

Menopause is usually reached between the ages of 45 and 55, with the average age being 51. Perimenopause tends to begin around mid-to-late-40s.

During perimenopause the amount of oestrogen within the body drops. It fluctuates, and it is this fluctuation that can cause a range of symptoms including, as is relevant for the purpose of this text:

- Hot flushes, which can come on rapidly and range in severity, all the way to feeling as if on fire;

- Night sweats;
- Sleep disturbances/disruption;
- Irregular menstrual periods including heavier or lighter bleeding;
- Mood swings, anxiety, irritability, depression;
- Memory problems and difficulty concentrating;
- Incontinence and increased risk of urinary tract infection;
- Increased risk of heart disease;
- Osteoporosis and increased risk of bone fracture.

Menopause in the workplace

There is no doubt that menopause can and does affect women in the workplace. Any of the above symptoms is likely to disrupt work performance, including requirements for medical visits in relation to some of the less-obviously-work-related problems (heart disease, osteoporosis).

Some of the symptoms such as hot flushes can be entirely disabling even if sporadic, and can take an employee out of the workplace for periods of time. Others will have a longer-term effect on work:

- Sleep disturbances and loss of concentration will likely affect productivity, and could lead to an increase in errors;
- Irregular, and perhaps unexpected, menstrual periods, heavier bleeding, and incontinence will cause more time away from the carrying out of the job role, perhaps through visits to the bathroom. They may also cause sudden departures from the workplace or particular job function;

- Memory problems may lead to errors and an increase in time needed to complete work. They can also have a social effect, and may give the impression of a lack of interest (as would concentration problems);

- Mood swings, anxiety, irritability, and depression may all cause a decrease in productivity. They can also cause passing alterations to personality, which may, in turn, affect interactions with colleagues and managers to the extent that those interactions might be deemed misconduct;

- As above, increased risk of heart disease and bone breakage is not likely to be an immediate problem, but may well result in more medical appointments and time out of work.

Employees experiencing menopause can, at least for the above reasons, be seen by some employers, unsympathetically, to disrupt workflow, affect team morale, and otherwise as someone not fulfilling their side of the contract of employment (to work, or to be ready, able, and willing to work). Currently, there is no specific legal protection for women experiencing menopause. It is theoretically possible to discriminate on the grounds of menopause. Menopause is not, of itself, a protected characteristic.

This book looks at how protections provided for by the existing law, specifically protection from discrimination and unfair dismissal, can apply to protect those experiencing menopause. It will consider which protected characteristics can apply to that situation, how various forms of discrimination can cover 'menopause discrimination', and how dismissals in relation to capability or conduct must be handled to ensure fairness.

# CHAPTER TWO

# MENOPAUSE AS A PROTECTED CHARACTERISTIC

Looking in more detail at the potential for 'menopause discrimination' requires us to identify a protected characteristic as provided for by s.4 Equality Act 2010, by reference to the further defining provisions contained within ss.5-12 Equality Act 2010. That much is obvious.

Equally obvious is that the clear candidates for applicable protected characteristics are sex, age, and disability insofar as menopause is uniquely feminine, applicable within a particular, albeit relatively broad, age range, and could potentially amount to a disability dependent on its effects. Conversely, it would affect women regardless of marital status, race, religion or belief, or sexual orientation.

Perhaps less obvious is that the protected characteristic of gender reassignment may well be in play in relation to a person experience menopause symptoms. For example, if a woman, as part of her transition to a man, was taking hormone blockers, she will experience menopause.

## Sex

Sex is defined, rather vaguely, by s.11(a) Equality Act 2010 as being:

> a reference to a person who has a particular protected characteristic is a reference to a man or to a woman.

The terms 'man' and 'woman' are defined in s.212(1) Equality Act 2010 respectively as:

> a male of any age and
>
> a female of any age.

It is recognised that there is some interaction between this provision and s.7 Equality Act 2010 (gender reassignment). The definitions of 'man' and 'woman' and the issue of how these apply to transgender persons are complex and beyond the scope of this text. The issues of sex and gender assignment and reassignment and consequent treatment in the workplace are important, but this book will not focus on them.

## Age

Age as a protected characteristic is not limited to the particular length of time that a person has lived. Rather, age is defined in the Equality Act 2010 as 'age group'. s.5(1)(a) Equality Act 2010 states:

> a reference to a person who has a particular protected characteristic is a reference to a person of a particular age group.

s.5(2) Equality Act 2010 adds that:

> A reference to an age group is a reference to a group of persons defined by reference to age, whether by reference to a particular age or to a range of age.

Whilst a single age can be set as a protected characteristic, a range of ages may also be. Certainly, it is more common for claimants to state an age group rather than a single age (for the obvious reason that it would be extremely difficult to prove that an employer is inclined to subject a person to a detriment because of their specific age, but would not do so were they one year older or younger).

The age group can be defined in any way. So, for example, it is legitimate to set it as 'over 70', 'under 30', or 'between 40 and 50'. This is particularly helpful in the case of someone experiencing menopause since they are likely to wish to identify their 'age' along the lines of 45-55. That would then capture the period within which menopause is more often, generally speaking, producing adverse effects. In other words, given that menopause is strongly linked with a particular age range, it might well be possible to say that treatment on the grounds of menopause or its symptoms is in fact treatment because of age.

Of course, by the same token, age as a relevant protected characteristic could have less straightforward applicability in the case of early or late onset of menopause. As the boundaries of the age group widen, the weaker the age/menopause association becomes in general terms. Consequently, it becomes more difficult to suggest that treatment on the ground of menopause is in fact because of a particular age group.

Disability

The definition of a disability is well-known, being (per s.6(1) Equality Act 2010):

> A 'physical or mental impairment' that
>
> Has 'a substantial and long-term adverse effect on P's ability to carry out normal day-to-day activities'.

A claimant must therefore be able to show the tribunal that:

1. They suffered from an impairment;
2. That impairment caused adverse effects on normal day-to-day activities;
3. Those adverse effects were substantial i.e. more than trivial;
4. Those adverse effects had been substantial in the long term i.e. they:
   (1) Had, at the time of the alleged act of discrimination, lasted at least 12 months;
   (2) Were, at the time of the alleged act of discrimination, likely to (in other words 'could well') last for at least 12 months or the rest of the claimant's life; or
   (3) Had ceased at the time of the alleged act of discrimination, but were likely to ('could well') recur as judged at the time of discrimination.

*Impairment*

It does not sit easily to equate menopause with impairment. When one thinks of impairment, one tends to imagine some form of damage or injury, or some form of reduction in bodily function. Menopause is entirely natural, and it could not realistically be said that the cessation of periods is, in itself, damage or injury.

However, it is not always necessary for a claimant to be able to point to a specific impairment (in the event of argument that 'menopause' was not an impairment as such). As the EAT stated in *J v. DLA Piper UK LLP* [2010] ICR 1052 at [38],

> There are indeed sometimes cases where identifying the nature of the impairment from which a claimant may be suffering involves difficult medical questions; and we agree that in many or most such cases it will be easier – and is entirely legitimate – for the tribunal to park that issue and to ask first whether the claimant's ability to carry out normal day-to-day activities has been adversely affected – one might indeed say 'impaired' – on a long-term basis. If it finds that it has been, it will in many or most cases follow as a matter of common sense inference that the claimant is suffering from a condition which has produced that adverse effect – in other words, an 'impairment'. If that inference can be drawn, it will be unnecessary for the tribunal to try to resolve difficult medical issues of the kind to which we have referred.

That is because, as the EAT stated in *Ministry of Defence v. Hay* [2008] ICR 1247 at [36], 'impairment' is not equated with 'clinical condition', and is a functional concept rather than a medical one.

*Substantial adverse effect*

The assessment of whether adverse effects are substantial is one of comparison of a claimant's abilities to carry out normal day-to-day activities with his or her ability had s/he not been impaired. Although the Office for Disability Issues, *Guidance on matters to be taken into account in determining questions relating to the definition of disability*, 2011 states at para. B1 that 'The requirement that an adverse effect on normal day-to-day activities should be a substantial one reflects the general understanding of disability as a limitation going beyond the normal differences in ability which may exist among people', the comparative exercise is not one of claimant against the average person (*Paterson v. Commissioner of Police of the Metropolis* [2007] ICR 1522).

Normal day-to-day activities are those activities that are done regularly by the general population, and do not necessarily need to be activities being done only by a particular individual. That extends to everyday activities done in the work environment, but does not include work-specialist activities.

Importantly, the focus for the tribunal is on what a claimant cannot do or can only do with difficulty, rather than what they can do. That was the error made by the tribunal in *Rooney v. Leicester City Council* UKEAT/0104/21. There, although the Claimant's evidence that, because of menopause, she suffered with memory loss, spent prolonged periods of time in bed because of fatigue/exhaustion, and experienced dizziness, incontinence, and joint pain was accepted by the tribunal, it found that she was able to carry out *some* day-to-day activities because she provided care to others. The EAT found that the tribunal had erred in focusing on what the claimant could do and weighed that against what she could not.

The tribunal must consider the effect of menopause as if no treatment (e.g. hormone replacement therapy) was being received.

Finally, and with potentially some significance, the tribunal must consider the cumulative effects of menopause as well as any individual effect. It may be that an individual effect is not, of itself, substantial. However, two or more together might substantially impair a person's ability to carry out normal day-to-day activities. Although not spelt out in terms by the tribunal in the case of *Donnachie v. Telent Technology Services Ltd.* case number 1300005/2020, it is apparent that that decision (that the claimant was disabled) was based on all the symptoms rather than any particular one.

*Long-term*

The issue that is most likely to affect someone experiencing menopause meeting the definition of disability is whether the effects are long-term. In many cases, there will have been a long-term substantial adverse effect on the individual at the time of the act(s) of discrimination. However, that will not always be the case. Whether the effects will last at least 12 months can only be measured at the date of the discriminatory act(s) and based on the information known at that date. The assessment cannot take account of events and information gained subsequent to the date of discrimination (see *Singapore Airlines Ltd. v. Casado-Guijarro* UKEAT/0386/13 for an example of the tribunal falling into that error).

It must be noted that it is the *effects* of menopause that must last 12 months or more, not the underlying cause. Someone may experience menopause, or any disability, without there being substantial adverse effects for the whole period of having the impairment. There is no disability if that impairment has been present for 12 months or more, but the effects only present at a substantial level for, say, six months.

Given that menopause can last for some years, this may be an issue that arises. The effects may not last, or may not be substantial for a sufficient period of time. If they have not, they may still be long-term if they recur or are likely to recur at a point beyond 12 months from the first occurrence. So, for example, someone that experiences effects in month one and month 14 may well be considered to be disabled, but someone that experiences effects in month one and month 10 would not.

Proving that the effects of menopause are/were likely to last, or recur beyond, 12 months at the time of an act of discrimination (assuming they had not already) might be a difficult issue for an employee to overcome. As with any disability, there is no guarantee, and medical evidence of some description to indicate that the effects 'could well' last or recur beyond 12 months may be required. Whilst it is perhaps not something capable of prognosing on a case-by-case basis, a GP letter, for example, stating that the employee in question is likely to experience the symptoms for 12 months is going to carry more weight than a number of internet searches demonstrating the average length of symptoms.

Overall, however, one would not expect the long-term issue to be too great a hurdle, but in some cases, employers could fairly put the employee to proof of the matter.

## Gender reassignment

s.7(1) Equality Act 2010 provides:

> A person has the protected characteristic of gender reassignment if the person is proposing to undergo, is undergoing or has undergone a process (or part of a process) for the purpose of reassigning the person's sex by changing physiological or other attributes of sex.

The issues of gender reassignment and its consequences are complex, and beyond the scope of this text. The effects of gender reassignment and consequent treatment in the workplace are important, but this book will focus on the menopause as impacted by the laws around sex, age, and disability discrimination.

## Summary

There is no clear-cut protection of the characteristic of menopause. The obvious candidate is the prohibition of disability discrimination in some circumstances. However, it will be seen that those experiencing menopause can derive some protection from the prohibition against sex and age discrimination; albeit that protection is not absolute.

# CHAPTER THREE

# DISCRIMINATION IN EMPLOYMENT

## Scope of this book

The aim of this book is to focus on the extent to which the laws of discrimination and unfair dismissal protect people experiencing menopause in the workplace. It will seek to outline various arguments that may apply in any discrimination or unfair dismissal claim. Some of those arguments, particularly in relation to disability discrimination will be more general since those claims are available in the case of any disability. However, since the purpose of this book is to consider the legal protections in the case of menopause, there are many areas of the law of discrimination and unfair dismissal that are non-specific to menopause, and are not necessary to consider.

Specifically, this book will not go into the following issue:

- Employment status
- Discrimination by association
- Victimisation
- Post-employment discrimination
- Vicarious and personal liability
- Time limits for tribunal claims
- Burden of proof
- Remedies

Discrimination against employees

The first task in any discrimination claim is to identify what it is that the employer is said to have done that amounts to discrimination, and whether that act is one potentially rendered unlawful by the Equality Act 2010, in particular s.39.

s.39 Equality Act 2010 sets out the following:

> (1) An employer (A) must not discriminate against a person (B)—
>
> > (a) in the arrangements A makes for deciding to whom to offer employment;
> >
> > (b) as to the terms on which A offers B employment;
> >
> > (c) by not offering B employment.
>
> (2) An employer (A) must not discriminate against an employee of A's (B)—
>
> > (a) as to B's terms of employment;
> >
> > (b) in the way A affords B access, or by not affording B access, to opportunities for promotion, transfer or training or for receiving any other benefit, facility or service;
> >
> > (c) by dismissing B;
> >
> > (d) by subjecting B to any other detriment.
>
> (3) An employer (A) must not victimise a person (B)—
>
> > (a) in the arrangements A makes for deciding to whom to offer employment;
> >
> > (b) as to the terms on which A offers B employment;
> >
> > (c) by not offering B employment.

(4) An employer (A) must not victimise an employee of A's (B)—

(a) as to B's terms of employment;

(b) in the way A affords B access, or by not affording B access, to opportunities for promotion, transfer or training or for any other benefit, facility or service;

(c) by dismissing B;

(d) by subjecting B to any other detriment.

...

(7) In subsections (2)(c) and (4)(c), the reference to dismissing B includes a reference to the termination of B's employment—

(a) by the expiry of a period (including a period expiring by reference to an event or circumstance);

(b) by an act of B's (including giving notice) in circumstances such that B is entitled, because of A's conduct, to terminate the employment without notice.

Without going into employment status to any great degree, it is at least important to note that an individual wishing to complain to the tribunal under s.39 Equality Act 2010 must be an applicant or employee. A self-employed contractor could not complain of discrimination. The concept of employee in the Equality Act 2010 (s.83(2)(a)) is wider than that in the Employment Rights Act 1996 and effectively mirrors the definition of worker in that Act (i.e. at s.230(3): someone who works or worked under (a) a contract of employment, or (b) any other contract, whether express or implied and (if it is express) whether oral or in writing, whereby the individual undertakes to do or perform personally any work or services for another party to the contract whose status is not by virtue of the contract that of a client or customer of any profession or business undertaking carried on by the individual).

In most cases, it will be simple to identify what the employer has done and that it is capable of amounting to unlawful discrimination. For instance, where someone is not promoted or dismissed, those acts are capable of being discriminatory (s.39(2)(b-c) Equality Act 2010), and the tribunal will assess whether the decision not to promote or to dismiss amounted to prohibited conduct under Part II Chapter II Equality Act 2010.

Not all acts of apparent discrimination are potentially unlawful. For example, it is ostensibly permissible to subject an applicant to a detriment. That is not included in s.39(1) Equality Act 2010 as something an employer must not do. In such a case, the question of whether there was, for example, direct discrimination of an applicant does not arise.

*Detriment*

The vast majority of intra-employment scenarios are covered by s.39(2) Equality Act 2010. However, in the case of any act falling outside s.39(2)(a-c) Equality Act 2010, before the question of discrimination arises, one must consider whether the act to which the employee was subjected amounted to a detriment. Not every act will. It is correct that the concept of 'any other detriment' is broad enough to capture acts of every nature. It is the severity of a particular act (or omission) that may affect determination of it as a detriment.

The accepted formulation is that a detriment 'exists if a reasonable worker would or might take the view that [the action of the employer] was in all the circumstances to his detriment' (*Ministry of Defence v. Jeremiah* [1980] ICR 13). However, the question is not entirely objective. The test in *Jeremiah*, it was said by Lord Scott in *Shamoon v. Chief Constable of the Royal Ulster Constabulary* [2003] UKHL 11 at [105], 'must be applied by considering the issue from the point of view of the victim. If the victim's opinion that the treatment was to his or her detriment is a reasonable one to hold, that ought…to suffice'. In other words, a justified and reasonable sense of grievance on the part of the employee can amount to a detriment, but an unjustified one cannot. Whether it is unjustified is, as established by *Shamoon*, a mixed subjective/objective test – not purely objective in that the employee must actually hold the sense of grievance before detriment is established.

The threshold over which an employee must cross before establishing that a detriment has been applied to them is undoubtedly low. That does not mean that s.39 Equality Act 2010 should be overlooked, and it could well be a point on which a marginal case turns.

# CHAPTER FOUR

# DISCRIMINATION IN RELATION TO ALL PROTECTED CHARACTERISTICS

## Direct discrimination

Direct discrimination is generally considered the most serious form of discrimination – it is treatment of an individual directed at their protected characteristic. Mostly, setting out such a claim is simple. In cases involving menopause, however, it is unlikely that treatment will be because of sex or age *per se*, but rather because of the menopause and/or its effects. That may easily permit a direct disability discrimination claim, dependent on qualification as disabled, but does not immediately identify sex or age discrimination. Those claims arise through an argument that menopause is intrinsic to those characteristics, and treatment because of it must therefore be regarded as treatment on the ground of sex and/or age. However, when one considers the nature of direct discrimination, which is to say that there must be a comparison between claimant and someone else in the same circumstances albeit not possessing the protected characteristic, it may be that effects of menopause should be applied to that comparator so that sex and/or age are to be isolated and their role (and their role alone) in the treatment assessed. Those competing arguments, and the viability of a direct discrimination claim in relation to menopause, are considered below.

s.13(1) Equality Act 2010 provides as follows:

> A person (A) discriminates against another (B) if, because of a protected characteristic, A treats B less favourably than A treats or would treat others.

*Comparators*

Direct discrimination is a comparative exercise. A tribunal must assess how an employee has been treated against how another person would be treated. That is, ultimately, the essence of discrimination, which is, after all, the act of distinguishing between one thing and another. A difference in treatment between individuals is therefore a fundamental aspect of s.13 Equality Act 2010 (indeed, the provision does not proscribe merely unfavourable treatment). The question of the reason for any particular treatment is, on the face of it, only half the test.

*Is a comparator necessary in a claim of direct discrimination?*

Whilst a comparison with another person, real or hypothetical is a requirement of s.13 Equality Act 2010, the higher courts have questioned whether construction of a comparator and testing favourability of treatment, before then considering the reason for the same, is always necessary. In *Shamoon v. Chief Constable of the Royal Ulster Constabulary* [2003] UKHL 11 at [8], Lord Nicholls said:

> No doubt there are cases where it is convenient and helpful to adopt this two-step approach to what is essentially a single question: did the claimant, on the proscribed ground, receive less favourable treatment than others? But, especially where the identity of the relevant comparator is a matter of dispute, this sequential analysis may give rise to needless problems. Sometimes the less favourable treatment issue cannot be resolved without, at the same time, deciding the reason why issue. The two issues are intertwined.

He went on to illustrate the point at [10]-[11]:

> 10. ...It is impossible to decide whether Chief Inspector Shamoon was treated less favourably than a hypothetical male chief inspector without identifying the ground on which she was treated as she was. Was it grounds of sex? If yes, then she was treated less favourably than a male chief inspector in her position would have been treated. If not, not. Thus, on this footing also, the less favourable treatment issue is incapable of being decided without

> deciding the reason why issue. And the decision on the reason why issue will also provide the answer to the less favourable treatment issue.
>
> 11. This analysis seems to me to point to the conclusion that employment tribunals may sometimes be able to avoid arid and confusing disputes about the identification of the appropriate comparator by concentrating primarily on why the claimant was treated as she was. Was it on the proscribed ground which is the foundation of the application? That will call for an examination of all the facts of the case. Or was it for some other reason? If the latter, the application fails. If the former, there will be usually be no difficulty in deciding whether the treatment, afforded to the claimant on the proscribed ground, was less favourable than was or would have been afforded to others.

In other words, both tests (less favourable treatment and reason) are two sides of the same coin, with the answer to one, in many cases, providing the answer to the other. As the EAT stated in *Law Society v. Bahl* [2003] IRLR 640 at [111], '...the finding that the treatment was on the grounds of race or sex will almost always involve a finding of less favourable treatment'. The EAT rejected the proposition that it was an error of law <u>not</u> to construct a hypothetical comparator and determine the treatment issue before considering the reason issue.

However, there will be cases where consideration of the comparator is useful, even if only to cross-check or assist the conclusion on whether a protected characteristic played any part in the treatment. Using a claim of sex discrimination based on menopause as an example, the tribunal may have difficulty in considering whether the alleged discriminator had a woman's sex in mind when they subjected her to a detriment, particularly where that detriment might have been because of the effects of menopause. It would not necessarily automatically follow from that reason that sex was the reason for treatment. Were a tribunal to ask whether, on the basis of the proven facts, a man would have been treated better in the same circumstances, that would, undoubtedly shed light on, if not resolve, the overall question of discrimination.

It would therefore, in appropriate cases, assist in reminding tribunals of a need to consider the comparator. As the EAT pointed out in *Bahl* at [114], '...whilst it is not necessary for tribunals to specify with precision the hypothetical comparator, they may find it helpful provisionally to try to do so in order to identify any potentially relevant explanations which might account for the difference in treatment. Whether they do account for it or not will depend upon the evidence which emerges during the trial' (see also *Stockton-on-Tees Borough Council v. Aylott* [2010] ICR 1278 at [45]: 'I am not saying that a hypothetical comparator can be dispensed with altogether in a case such as this: it is part of the process of identifying the ground of the treatment and it is good practice to cross check by constructing a hypothetical comparator').

*Who is an appropriate comparator?*

If a comparator *is* to be used in a given case, thought must be given to the identity of that person, and how well they reflect the circumstances of the claimant in question.

s.23(1) Equality Act 2010 provides:

> On a comparison of cases for the purposes of section 13, 14, or 19 there must be no material difference between the circumstances relating to each case.

To put it another way, one must compare 'like with like' (*Shamoon v. Chief Constable of the Royal Ulster Constabulary* [2003] UKHL 11 at [46]). That does not mean, however, that the comparator must be a clone of the claimant. As the EHRC Code points out at [3.23], '...it is not necessary for the circumstances of the two people (that is, the worker and the comparator) to be identical in every way; what matters is that the circumstances which are relevant to the treatment of the worker are the same or nearly the same for the worker and the comparator'. The 'circumstances relating to each case' in s.23 Equality Act 2010 'are those which the alleged discriminator takes into account when deciding to treat the woman as he does or when deciding to treat the man as he treats, or would treat, him' (*Shamoon* at [134]).

So, if a woman with, for example, one year's service is dismissed for menopause-related absences, her length of service may be a factor shared by a male comparator, but if the length of service did not bear on the decision to dismiss, it need not be shared – it was not a circumstance relating to the case and is irrelevant (it may also mean that a finding of less favourable treatment would always follow (see *Madden v. Preferred Technical Group CHA Ltd.* [2004] EWCA Civ 1178)).

In that vein, the EAT provided guidance in *Kalu v. Brighton and Sussex University Hospitals NHS Trust* UKEAT/0609/12 at [24]:

> The concept of '*relevant* circumstances' requires identification of that to which the circumstances in question are relevant: there must be a sufficient link in logic between the two if the Tribunal's conclusion of fact is to stand...The purpose of making the comparison thus needs to be understood before a comparator may properly be identified. It may often be convenient to address selection of the relevant circumstances by asking what proposition the comparison is intended to address. Where, for instance, it is that one of two candidates was favoured by discrimination over another for a job, the circumstances will be those which relate to suitability for employment in it. If one is shown to live miles away from the intended place of work, and the other close by, this may be a relevant circumstance if, for instance, the job may involve a rapid out-of-hours response from the appointee. It may not be so if the 'place of work' is in reality a base from which to travel to assignments...As the judgments in *Shamoon* articulate, if the reason for the appointment is because of the ready availability of the successful candidate, compared to the travel difficulties that would be suffered by the disappointed one, it would be unnecessary to address whether this was a relevant circumstance (it would almost certainly not be related to any protected characteristic), and whether it was different as between the claimant and the proposed comparator – if so there would be an answer to the claim. But if not approached by that route, and if instead the identification of a comparator is relied on to help the Tribunal decide what was the reason that one candidate succeeded and the other did not, the answer would be that in the context of the particular issues before

> the Tribunal it would be a relevant circumstance, and the position of the two could not properly be compared. The disappointed candidate would have to ask – how would the hypothetical comparator, someone with my personal characteristics, save for the one in question, but living miles away from the intended place of work have been treated?

It is frequently the case that real-life comparators identified by a claimant are not in sufficiently materially similar circumstances to qualify. A hypothetical comparator will instead be adopted, but the real-life comparator will still serve some use. The tribunal should be able to use them as an evidential comparator, albeit having due regard to the differences in circumstances, in order to come to a conclusion as to how a hypothetical comparator would have been treated.

An interesting question, that will no doubt develop as cases involving direct discrimination arising from menopause begin to increase in number, is that of the correct comparator, and, in particular, whether any of the symptoms of menopause should be shared by that comparator. Certainly, where treatment is because of, say, specifically illness caused by menopause (as opposed to a wider problem such as performance or attendance), the easy answer to the question is that the comparator must have experienced the same illness, albeit not related to menopause. An employer would then (probably successfully) argue that the comparator would have been treated in the same way given the illness was the focus for that treatment.

That would meet the accepted approach of the EAT in *High Quality Lifestyles Ltd. v. Watts* [2006] IRLR 850. There, the claimant was HIV positive. He worked for the respondent as a support worker. When he disclosed his condition some months after starting employment, he was told that he was considered high-risk (of transmitting HIV). Around that time, he had 'received on six separate days scratches, superficial abrasions, deep lacerations and a bite from different service users'. He was dismissed and claimed that his dismissal was an act of direct discrimination. This is perhaps an example of a case in which it appeared clear that the reason for dismissal was disability, but it did not automatically follow that the claimant was treated less favourably than someone in materially the same circumstances would have been, and therefore that part of the test needed consideration. The EAT said of the comparator at [48] (emphasis added):

> The error which the Tribunal made in paragraphs 84 and 85 of its reasons was in failing to impute relevant circumstances to the hypothetical comparator. The circumstances were not, as the Tribunal found, that the comparator should have a communicable disease. Assuming, as the Tribunal correctly did, that the comparator has the same 'abilities, skills and experience', <u>the comparator must also have some attribute, whether caused by a medical condition or otherwise, which is not HIV+. This attribute must carry the same risk of causing to others illness or injury of the same gravity, here serious and possibly fatal</u>. If the Tribunal found that the comparator would have been dismissed, then the Claimant has not been less favourably treated.

In other words, the comparator's relevant circumstances, including the effects of the disability, must be so closely matched to the claimant's so that only the specific disability giving rise to the effects is the differentiation. In isolating the protected characteristic as the distinguishing feature in this way, one could arguably claim that the less favourable treatment test is narrowed so far that it becomes irrelevant. It could be said that it is the reason for treatment test by another means, in that if the only difference between the comparator and claimant is the protected characteristic, the only question to ask is whether that caused the treatment.

That will plainly reduce the scope of applicability of s.13 Equality Act 2010 to a menopause age and/or sex discrimination case (and a disability case). If, in the case of dismissal or detriment for menopause-related illness, a hypothetical man, or hypothetical younger man or woman, were to be ascribed all the adverse effects of menopause, but not menopause itself, it is almost inevitable that the comparator would be treated in the same way (although direct disability discrimination may well follow in appropriate cases). In the case of wider causes of detriment or dismissal such as performance or attendance, it may be less clear that a comparator would be treated better because the focus would be on the performance/attendance rather than the causative illness. Identification of the alleged discriminator's thought-processes are important, as set out above.

Where it can be identified that the thought-processes of an alleged discriminator include detriment because of, specifically, menopause itself, or menopause-related illness, it could be suggested that the comparator does not similarly suffer. Whilst accepting that the comparator is an artificial construct, it is almost too artificial to suggest that a hypothetical man, or other person outside the relevant age range, suffers from menopause-related illness. There is support for such an approach. In *Stockton-on-Tees Borough Council v. Aylott* [2010] ICR 1278 at [47], the EAT said that (emphasis added):

> ...some of the claimant's particular behavioural and performance difficulties and his move to another post stemmed from his particular disability. The employment tribunal are not, and cannot be, criticised for leaving the claimant's particular disability out of the circumstances of the hypothetical comparator. Section 3A(5) [Disability Discrimination Act 1995] stipulates that the comparator does not have the disability. In my judgment, <u>there was no error in the employment tribunal also leaving out of those circumstances particular results caused by the claimant's disability: the move to another post and the behavioural and performance difficulties resulting from the particular disability would not be relevant circumstances of a hypothetical comparator who did not have that particular disability</u>.

If it were accepted that menopause and its attendant effects are inherently sex-related and age-related, or at the least 'stem from' sex and/or age, *Aylott* would suggest that they not be shared by the comparator. It goes without saying that the same would apply to disability.

The point is also illustrated in the case of *Lockwood v. Department of Work and Pensions* [2013] IRLR 941. There, the claimant applied for voluntary redundancy. She was 26 at the time. At that age and with eight years' service, she was entitled to a payment of £10,849 under the Civil Service Compensation Scheme. However, had she been over 35, she would have received £17,691. She claimed that that was direct age discrimination. The tribunal dismissed the claim, finding that the age groups were materially different, on the basis that 'the evidence showed that individuals in the younger categories and in their 20s, who had lesser financial and family obligations, could generally be expected to react more easily and rapidly to the loss of their jobs and greater flexibility could be expected of them. They were also more likely to move into employment than older people'.

The Court of Appeal overturned the decision. It said at [37]-[38]:

> 37. It instead approached the case by bringing into account in its assessment of the relevant circumstances the fact that, because Ms Lockwood was younger than the comparator and belonged to a generation whose members could adjust more easily and rapidly to the loss of jobs than their colleagues in their late 30s, her circumstances were materially different from those of the comparator.
>
> 38. Those considerations were, however, nothing more than features of being 26 rather than 36. The ET's reasoning appears to have been that, because a 26-year-old leaver can be assumed not to need as much money as a 36-year-old leaver, there was no less favourable treatment in giving the former a lower severance payment than the latter. Even if the premise was correct, the conclusion was self-evidently wrong. The premise, if right, may have provided grounds for justifying the disparity of the treatment between the different age groups. But that was a different question. There was, however, no question that Ms Lockwood suffered less favourable treatment than her comparator. The ET ought so to have found, and the EAT was wrong in failing to correct its error.

As Lewison LJ put it at [57]:

> When she left her job Ms Lockwood received less money than a 36-year-old would have received. Why? The answer is: because she was younger. The ET said that the statistics showed that someone like Ms Lockwood would be able to react more easily and rapidly to losing her job than a 36-year-old. Why? The answer again is: because she was younger. They also said that someone like Ms Lockwood would be less likely to have heavy financial

> responsibilities than a 36-year-old. Why? The answer yet again is: because she was younger. Accordingly all the suggested reasons for concluding that Ms Lockwood did not suffer age discrimination turn out to be factors consequent upon her age. They are, therefore, not legitimate differences for the purpose of deciding whether discrimination has taken place.

In other words, although this case specifically deals with the issue of whether or not a comparator was valid where they were in an ostensibly different position from the claimant, one can assert, in light of the rationale, that a male comparator without menopause-related illness/symptoms is valid. Those effects are the consequence of sex and/or age, and not ascribing them to the comparator would not make the latter materially different.

Finally, there may be some support to be drawn by way of analogy with pregnancy cases; in particular, earlier decisions surrounding the issue of whether discrimination on the grounds of pregnancy was in fact sex discrimination, and against whom must the female claimant be compared. In *Webb v. EMO Air Cargo (UK) Ltd.* [1994] ICR 770, the ECJ stated at [24]-[25] that:

> 24. …there can be no question of comparing the situation of a woman who finds herself incapable, by reason of pregnancy discovered very shortly after the conclusion of the employment contract, of performing the task for which she was recruited with that of a man similarly incapable for medical or other reasons.
>
> 25. As Mrs Webb rightly argues, pregnancy is not in any way comparable with a pathological condition, and even less so with unavailability for work on non-medical grounds, both of which are situations that may justify the dismissal of a woman without discriminating on grounds of sex. Moreover, in the Hertz judgment, cited above, the Court drew a clear distinction between pregnancy and illness…

Where, therefore, a claimant is experiencing something inherently related to her sex and age, it is arguable that the question of comparator becomes simple – a man or younger man/woman not suffering the adverse effects of menopause. However, the pregnancy analogy is not without difficulty. The ECJ was determining the comparator question in the context of other legislation (the Pregnancy Workers Directive) that provided 'special protection' for pregnant women and their health and safety. There is no such legislation applicable to those experiencing menopause.

Second, the rationale for excluding the comparison with a sick man is the distinction between protecting the 'biological condition' of a woman during and after pregnancy, and otherwise handling 'pathological conditions'. It was recognised at [21] that, for the former group, there were '...harmful effects which the risk of dismissal may have on the physical and mental state of women who are pregnant, have recently given birth or are breastfeeding, including the particularly serious risk that pregnant women may be prompted voluntarily to terminate their pregnancy' hence the introduction of the Pregnant Workers Directive. It could be said, with some legitimacy, that menopause is a pathological condition, distinct from pregnancy, and that the same type of protection is not required. Therefore, as an analogy, it might well not be workable.

*Summary: comparators*

The issue of comparators can be a technical and complex one. It may not be necessary in a given case, but useful in another. There are competing arguments as to the relevant applicable characteristics in a 'menopause discrimination' case, which make those cases either easier or more difficult to succeed. The traditional approach of ascribing all the claimant's characteristics to the comparator may not be appropriate, but may be difficult to surmount, and developments in the law will be watched with interest.

*Less favourable treatment*

It is important to identify that a claimant has been treated less favourably than another person was or would be. There is a number of guiding principles that assist in determining whether less favourable treatment has occurred. They can be simply stated as set out below.

It is for the tribunal to decide whether a claimant has been treated less favourably than a comparator. That is an objective question: it does not matter whether the claimant believes there has been less favourable treatment (*Burrett v. West Birmingham Health Authority* [1994] IRLR 7).

It also does not matter that the alleged discriminator believed they were conferring an advantage, if the treatment is objectively less favourable (*Chief Constable of Devon and Cornwall Police v. Town* [2021] IRLR 235).

An employer cannot offset less favourable treatment with some form of consideration for it (*Ministry of Defence v. Jeremiah* [1980] ICR 13).

Different treatment, without more, is not less favourable treatment (*Chief Constable of West Yorkshire Police v. Khan* [2001] ICR 1065).

The bare facts of different treatment alongside a difference in status is not sufficient to conclude that there has been discrimination (*Madarassay v. Nomura International plc* [2007] ICR 867).

Unreasonable treatment alone is not less favourable treatment (*Glasgow City Council v. Zafar* [1998] ICR 120).

However, the absence of an explanation for unreasonable treatment might imply less favourable treatment of the claimant when compared with a comparator (*Igen Ltd. v. Wong* [2005] ICR 931).

Further, a tribunal may not accept that the unreasonable conduct would be applied to the comparator where the employer had no good reason to do so (see *Eagle Place Services Ltd. v. Rudd* [2010] IRLR 486 where it would have been wholly unreasonable to dismiss a comparator for what would have been an irrational reason, where the comparator would not have been seen as an 'inconvenient liability').

In any event, the unreasonableness of treatment can go to credibility, in that the tribunal is more likely to reject the employer's explanation for the treatment if it is more unreasonable and *vice versa* (*Bahl v. Law Society* [2003] IRLR 640).

A good example of the latter principle in action is in *Merchant v. British Telecommunications plc* case number 1401305/2011. The claimant was dismissed because of performance concerns. The respondent, however, failed to investigate whether or not the claimant's menopause impacted on her performance. Contrary to the usual procedure, the employer did not refer the claimant for medical assessment. The tribunal found that the dismissing officer's explanation for that was 'irrational' and did 'not follow any logic', and was contrary to what he had written in a contemporaneous document. The explanation, which was that he relied on what he knew of his wife's menopause and that of the HR advisor, also demonstrated that he had made assumptions about the claimant's menopause. It was this explanation (and rejecting it as not credible) that led the tribunal to conclude that the dismissing officer had treated the claimant less favourably than he would a man in the same position.

*Causation: reason for treatment*

Demonstrating that a comparator would be or would have been treated more favourably is not sufficient to establish discrimination – the treatment must be <u>because of</u> the protected characteristic.

There are two ways in which treatment can be because of a protected characteristic. The EAT explained the test in *Amnesty International v. Ahmed* [2009] ICR 1450 at [32]-[36]:

> 32. …The basic question in a direct discrimination case is what is or are the 'ground' or 'grounds' for the treatment complained of. That is the language of the definitions of direct discrimination in the main discrimination statutes and the various more recent employment equality regulations. It is also the terminology used in the underlying Directives: see, e g, article 2(2)(a) of Directive 2000/43/EC ('the Race Directive') (OJ 2000 L180, p 22). There is however no difference between that formulation and asking what was the 'reason' that the act complained of was done, which is the language used in the victimisation provisions (e.g. section 2(1) of the 1976 Act): see per Lord Nicholls in *Nagarajan v London Regional Transport* [1999] ICR 877, 886 a–b (also, to the same effect, Lord Steyn, at p 894 f – g).
>
> 33. In some cases the ground, or the reason, for the treatment complained of is inherent in the act itself. If an owner of premises puts up a sign saying 'no blacks admitted', race is, necessarily, the

> ground on which (or the reason why) a black person is excluded. *James v Eastleigh Borough Council* [1990] ICR 554 is a case of this kind...In cases of this kind what was going on inside the head of the putative discriminator—whether described as his intention, his motive, his reason or his purpose—will be irrelevant. The 'ground' of his action being inherent in the act itself, no further inquiry is needed...
>
> 34. But that is not the only kind of case. In other cases—of which *Nagarajan* is an example—the act complained of is not in itself discriminatory but is rendered so by a discriminatory motivation, i.e. by the 'mental processes' (whether conscious or unconscious) which led the putative discriminator to do the act. Establishing what those processes were is not always an easy inquiry, but tribunals are trusted to be able to draw appropriate inferences from the conduct of the putative discriminator and the surrounding circumstances (with the assistance where necessary of the burden of proof provisions). Even in such a case, however, it is important to bear in mind that the subject of the inquiry is the ground of, or reason for, the putative discriminator's action, not his motive: just as much as in the kind of case considered in *James v Eastleigh Borough Council*, a benign motive is irrelevant...
>
> ...
>
> 36. There is thus, we think, no real difficulty in reconciling *James v Eastleigh Borough Council* and *Nagarajan v London Regional Transport*. In the analyses adopted in both cases, the ultimate question is—necessarily—what was the ground of the treatment complained of (or—if you prefer—the reason why it occurred). The difference between them simply reflects the different ways in which conduct may be discriminatory.

Lady Hale explained the former example (criterion cases) further (which explanation should be useful in menopause-based criterion cases, should they arise) in *Essop v. Home Office* [2017] IRLR 558, when she stated at [17] (emphasis added):

> *James v Eastleigh Borough Council* also shows that, even if the protected characteristic is not the overt criterion, there will still be direct discrimination if the criterion used (in that case retirement age) exactly corresponds with a protected characteristic (in that case sex) and is thus a proxy for it.

An example of this is the case of *Ball and another v. Hull and another* [2012] UKSC 73 where the defendants, who ran a small hotel, restricted double-bedded rooms to married couples. That was to accord with their own religious beliefs that homosexual relations, and heterosexual relations outside marriage, were sinful. The defendants refused to honour the claimants' booking of a double room. The claimants were a homosexual couple in a civil partnership. Although the defendants argued that the criterion that only *married* couples would be permitted a double room meant that it was not the claimants' sexuality that was the basis for the decision (it similarly applied to heterosexual unmarried couples), the Supreme Court held that civil partnership was in all respects indistinguishable from marriage in law. It said at [30] (emphasis added):

> When it came to denying a double bed to Mr Preddy and Mr Hall, which they would have given to a heterosexual married couple, Mr and Mrs Bull were not only applying the criterion that they were unmarried. They were applying a criterion that their legal relationship was not that of one man and one woman, in other words a criterion indistinguishable from sexual orientation.

If an employer were to have some criterion such as not recruiting anyone experiencing menopause, or due to experience menopause, there is at least an argument that that is indistinguishable from sex and age, and is thus inherently directly discriminatory. That is likely to be a rare scenario, but not impossible in a given case once all the evidence of the employer's practices is before the tribunal.

An express criterion is not necessary; it is still a requirement for the tribunal to determine what, if any, criterion was adopted by the employer (see *Onu v. Akwiwu* [2016] ICR 756).

The process for the tribunal is as follows. Addressing the factual criteria applied by the alleged discriminator in reaching his decision to treat the employee as s/he did is the first step. The tribunal would look to whether any criterion was applied, and, if so, whether it was based on a protected characteristic. Only if the factual criteria are not plain is it then necessary to explore the mental processes of the alleged discriminator so as to discover what facts (not motivation) led him/her to discriminate. The full explanation of this analytical process is to be found in *R (E) v. Governing Body of JFS and the admissions appeal panel of JFS* [2010] IRLR 136 at [21]-[23].

Where there is no plain criterion or criteria applied by the employer, and the case is a so-called 'mental processes' case, the tribunal must ask why the alleged discriminator acted as they did. It must seek to determine what the conscious or unconscious reason was (see *Chief Constable of West Yorkshire Police v. Khan* [2001] ICR 1065).

Decisions based on stereotypes or assumptions will, depending on the circumstances, be directly discriminatory. In *Coleman v. Skyrail Oceanic Ltd.* [1981] ICR 864, two employees of competing companies married each other. The two employers decided between themselves that the employment of one of them could not continue, and the female employee was dismissed because it was assumed that the male employee was the breadwinner. That was direct sex discrimination. The key issue was whether the dismissing employer would have treated a man in the same way, and their assumption showed that they would not.

In the same way, in *Merchant v. British Telecommunications plc* case number 1401305/2011, referred to under 'less favourable treatment' above, there was direct discrimination where the employer made generalised assumptions about menopause, including that the claimant could not improve her performance.

Similarly, an employer that mistakenly believes that an employee is going through menopause and treats them less favourably, subject to the comparator issue, because of that belief, can be found to have committed direct discrimination.

However, there must be evidence from which it could be inferred that assumptions were made about a claimant, and that those assumptions operated on the mind of the employer (see *Stockton-on-Tees Borough Council v. Aylott* [2010] ICR 1278 at [49]).

Similarly, there must be evidence from primary and surrounding facts showing that a protected characteristic was the reason for treatment. In *Talbot v. Costain Oil, Gas and Process Ltd.* [2017] ICR D11, the EAT summarised the principles from the authorities at [15]:

> (1) It is very unusual to find direct evidence of discrimination;
>
> (2) Normally the Tribunal's decision will depend on what inference it is proper to draw from all the relevant surrounding circumstances, which will often include conduct by the alleged discriminator before and after the unfavourable treatment in question;
>
> (3) It is essential that the Tribunal makes findings about any 'primary facts' which are in issue so that it can take them into account as part of the relevant circumstances;
>
> (4) The Tribunal's assessment of the parties and their witnesses when they give evidence forms an important part of the process of inference;
>
> (5) Assessing the evidence of the alleged discriminator when giving an explanation for any treatment involves an assessment not only of credibility but also reliability, and involves testing the evidence by reference to objective facts and documents, possible motives and the overall probabilities; and, where there are a number of allegations of discrimination involving one personality, conclusions about that personality are obviously going to be relevant in relation to all the allegations;
>
> (6) The Tribunal must have regard to the totality of the relevant circumstances and give proper consideration to factors which point towards discrimination in deciding what inference to draw in relation to any particular unfavourable treatment;

> (7) If it is necessary to resort to the burden of proof in this context, section 136 of the Equality Act 2010 provides in effect that where it would be proper to draw an inference of discrimination in the absence of 'any other explanation' the burden lies on the alleged discriminator to prove there was no discrimination.

*Justification: direct age discrimination*

Direct discrimination cannot be justified other than in the case of direct age discrimination. Justification is defined as a proportionate means of achieving a legitimate aim (s.13(2) Equality Act 2010). For further guidance on justification, see the paragraphs in relation to indirect discrimination and discrimination arising from disability below. There is one important difference between justification of direct age discrimination and justifying either indirect discrimination or discrimination arising from disability. That is that the legitimate aim must be of a public interest nature. The Supreme Court summarised two categories of legitimate aim in *Seldon v. Clarkson Wright & Jakes* [2012] ICR 716 at [56]-[57]:

> 56. ...The first kind may be summed up as *inter-generational fairness*...It can mean a variety of things, depending upon the particular circumstances of the employment concerned: for example, it can mean facilitating access to employment by young people; it can mean enabling older people to remain in the workforce; it can mean sharing limited opportunities to work in a particular profession fairly between the generations; it can mean promoting diversity and the interchange of ideas between younger and older workers.
>
> 57. The second kind may be summed up as *dignity*. This has been variously put as avoiding the need to dismiss older workers on the grounds of incapacity or underperformance, thus preserving their dignity and avoiding humiliation, and as avoiding the need for costly and divisive disputes about capacity or underperformance...

As to examples of what might be a legitimate aim for the purpose of justifying direct age discrimination, the supplement to the EHRC Code states at [3.4.2]:

> Legitimate aims can be summarised as promoting inter-generational fairness and 'dignity' and may include:
>
> - promoting access to employment for younger people
> - the efficient planning of the departure and recruitment of staff
> - sharing out employment opportunities fairly between the generations
> - ensuring the mix of generations of staff so as to promote the exchange of experience and new ideas
> - rewarding experience
> - cushioning the blow for long-serving employees who may find it hard to find new employment if dismissed
> - facilitating the participation of older workers in the workforce.

*Summary: direct discrimination*

The difficulty with direct discrimination is that, in most cases, treatment of an employee is likely to be because of something relating to menopause (meaning that a man or younger woman having done the same thing will likely be treated in the same way). Even if it is because of menopause itself, there is a question over whether that means there has been sex or age discrimination (if menopause is a disability, direct disability discrimination likely follows). The question of comparators could be central to that point, and there may well be or need to be development of the law to reflect the fact of menopause being inherently sex and age-related.

## Indirect discrimination

Indirect discrimination is the opposite of direct discrimination in that, rather than isolate an individual for particular treatment, an employer, through a particular policy for example, treats every person in the same way. However, for indirect discrimination to take place, it is that generic treatment that creates a disadvantage for a group of people sharing a particular protected characteristic when compared with a group not sharing it. Again, the focus is on the discriminatory effect on the specific characteristic (age, sex, disability). If the effect of an employer's policy has a greater impact on someone experiencing menopause, a question arises as to whether that can amount to indirect discrimination on the grounds of, particularly age or sex, where the impact is not on those characteristics *per se.*

The assessment, in an indirect discrimination claim, is of the effect of an employer's policy or practice. The policies or practices that can impact those experiencing menopause are wide and varied. It is not possible to list all the imaginable requirements held by an employer and assess the applicability of 'menopause discrimination' in all those cases. The majority of what follows is to set out the key features of indirect discrimination, as it would apply to menopause, but is sufficiently general to apply in wider circumstances.

s.19 Equality Act 2010 states as follows:

> (1) A person (A) discriminates against another (B) if A applies to B a provision, criterion or practice which is discriminatory in relation to a relevant protected characteristic of B's.
>
> (2) For the purposes of subsection (1), a provision, criterion or practice is discriminatory in relation to a relevant protected characteristic of B's if—
>
> > (a) A applies, or would apply, it to persons with whom B does not share the characteristic,

(b) it puts, or would put, persons with whom B shares the characteristic at a particular disadvantage when compared with persons with whom B does not share it,

(c) it puts, or would put, B at that disadvantage, and

(d) A cannot show it to be a proportionate means of achieving a legitimate aim.

(3) The relevant protected characteristics are—

- age;
- disability;
- gender reassignment;
- marriage and civil partnership;
- race;
- religion or belief;
- sex;
- sexual orientation.

*Provision, criterion, or practice*

The Equality Act 2010 does not define provision, criterion, or practice ('PCP'). The EHRC Code says at [4.5] that the term 'should be construed widely so as to include, for example, any formal or informal policies, rules, practices, arrangements, criteria, conditions, prerequisites, qualifications or provisions'.

Below are applicable principles when considering PCPs.

A PCP does not have to be an 'absolute bar' to something, and a PCP can allow for exceptions (*British Airways plc v. Starmer* [2005] IRLR 862).

'The words 'provision, criterion or practice' are not terms of art, but are ordinary English words…they are broad and overlapping, and in light of the object of the legislation, not to be narrowly construed or unjustifiably limited in their application' (*Ishola v. Transport for London* [2020] IRLR 368 at [35]).

There is no need to determine whether 'that which provides discrimination is a 'provision' on the one hand, a 'criterion' on the other or a 'practice' on the next: the question for the Tribunal is whether apparent discrimination results from something which might properly be described by any or all of those labels and if so whether it can be justified' (*Chief Constable of West Midlands Police v. Harrod* [2017] IRLR 539 at [23]).

A one-off decision can be a PCP (*British Airways plc v. Starmer* [2005] IRLR 862). However, not all one-off decisions are PCPs – 'all three words [provision, criterion, practice] carry the connotation of a state of affairs (whether framed positively or negatively and however informal) indicating how similar cases are generally treated or how a similar case would be treated if it occurred again…'practice' here connotes some form of continuum in the sense that it is the way in which things generally are or will be done. That does not mean it is necessary for the PCP or 'practice' to have been applied to anyone else in fact. Something may be a practice or done 'in practice' if it carries with it an indication that it will or would be done again in future if a hypothetical similar case arises' (*Ishola v. Transport for London* [2020] IRLR 368 at [38]).

A practice does not have to be universally followed in order to be a PCP, it need only be something that is a 'general or habitual approach' (*Williams v. Governing Body of Alderman Davies Church in Wales Primary School* [2020] IRLR 589 at [80]).

Not every act of unfair treatment of an employee amounts to a PCP. 'If an employer unfairly treats an employee by an act or decision and neither direct discrimination nor disability related discrimination is made out because the act or decision was not done/made by reason of disability or other relevant ground, it is artificial and wrong to seek to convert them by a process of abstraction into the application of a discriminatory PCP' (*Ishola v. Transport for London* [2020] IRLR 368 at [37]).

A dismissal, of itself, is unlikely to amount to a PCP. Rather it is likely to be the result of the application of a PCP (*Fox v. British Airways plc* UKEAT/0315/14).

A PCP must be identified with precision so as not to invalidate the claim (see *Francis v. British Airways Engineering Overhaul Ltd.* [1982] IRLR 10 where the terms of the PCP pleaded resulted in a claim based on an alleged requirement of the employer's that did not in fact exist).

The PCP must actually have been applied to the claimant (*Iteshi v. General Council of the Bar* UKEAT/0161/11).

It is not necessary that the PCP actually was applied to others, what is required is to extrapolate it to others i.e. determine the effect had it been applied to those others (*British Airways plc v. Starmer* [2005] IRLR 862 at [18]).

The time of the application of the PCP must also be identified, if for no other reason than tribunal time limits. The time to assess the employee's ability to comply with a condition is the date on which the employee must have complied with it (*Commission for Racial Equality v. Dutton* [1989] IRLR 8).

*Comparison with persons not sharing protected characteristic*

Once the PCP is identified, the next step under s.19 Equality Act 2010 is to establish that it 'puts, or would put, persons with whom B shares the characteristic at a particular disadvantage <u>when compared with persons with whom B does not share it</u>'. That is plainly a comparative exercise. It is an exercise that, unlike direct discrimination, which is a comparison between a claimant and a particular individual, sets groups of people against each other.

The accepted method of testing the PCP is to consider a pool of people within which there will be two groups for comparison: one made up of people sharing the claimant's protected characteristic, and one not sharing it.

Guidance on constructing the appropriate pool for comparison is as follows.

s.23 Equality Act 2010 applies to the comparison for the purposes of s.19 Equality Act 2010, which is to say that the comparator groups must be in materially the same relevant circumstances.

'In general, the pool should consist of the group which the provision, criterion or practice affects (or would affect) either positively or negatively, while excluding workers who are not affected by it, either positively or negatively' (EHRC Code at [4.18]).

'There is no warrant for including only some of the persons affected by the PCP for comparison purposes. In general, therefore, identifying the PCP will also identify the pool for comparison' (*Essop v. Home Office* [2017] IRLR 558 at [41]).

A pool should therefore not be limited by any sub-division of the group affected by the PCP (see *Jones v. University of Manchester* [1993] IRLR 218 where the PCP affected graduates, so that the pool could not be defined as 'graduate in a particular subject' or 'mature graduates').

Similarly, a pool should not be so wide as to include irrelevant persons: 'The identity of the appropriate pool will depend upon identifying that sector of the relevant workforce which is affected or potentially affected by the application of the particular requirement or condition in question and the context or circumstances in which it is sought to be applied. In this case, the pool was all those members of the employer's workforce, namely train operators, to whom the new rostering arrangements were to be applied…It did not include all the employer's employees. Nor did the pool extend to include the wider field of potential new applicants to the employer for a job as a train operator. That is because the discrimination complained of was the requirement for *existing* employees to enter into a new contract embodying the rostering arrangement; it was not a complaint brought by an applicant from outside complaining about the terms of the job applied for' (*London Underground Ltd. v. Edwards (No. 2)* [1999] ICR 494 at [23]).

Where an employee experiencing menopause is considering the discriminatory effect of a PCP therefore, they must look to all those people of all ages, sexes, those experiencing and not experiencing menopause, to whom the PCP is relevant. Unlike direct discrimination, where a claimant can define the comparator so as to ask how treatment would have differed in their case, if at all, an indirect discrimination claim simply asks how the PCP affects women as against men, or those in a particular age group as against those younger (or older). It is arguably artificial to create a pool of 'all those suffering from menopause symptoms' since that restricts the pool to a sub-division of all those affected by a PCP. Although the possible scenarios are infinite and too vast to list here, there will be a great deal of thought required in creating a pool so that it meets the above requirements but highlights, through menopause, an inevitable discriminatory impact on age and sex. It may well be that that pool simply does not exist in a given case.

The same can probably not be said where menopause is relied on as a disability. A claimant in that case can align themselves with all those people suffering similarly and compare that group to those not suffering at all i.e. without the disability. Menopause, in that case, is the protected characteristic and the comparison exercise is straightforward, and is not between characteristics in which some of those possessing the same may or may not be impaired by menopause.

*Particular disadvantage*

Once an appropriate pool is identified, a tribunal will assess whether the PCP affects, in a menopause case, women more than men, a particular age group more than another, disabled employees more than non-disabled employees.

It is first useful to understand how the phrase 'particular disadvantage' is used.

The EHRC Code at [4.9] suggests 'It could include denial of an opportunity or choice, deterrence, rejection or exclusion. The courts have found that 'detriment', a similar concept, is something that a reasonable person would complain about'.

'Particular disadvantage' does not require any particular level or threshold (*Pendleton v. Derbyshire County Council* [2016] IRLR 580 at [33]. It must not be misunderstood that 'particular disadvantage' means that only a particularly serious disadvantage would give grounds for a finding of indirect discrimination. The wording means that indirect discrimination must be taken to exist wherever an apparently neutral provision, criterion or practice affects certain persons – e.g. members of a certain racial or ethnic group – more adversely than others. The seriousness of the disadvantage can be relevant at most in considering justification: the more serious the disadvantage, the higher the requirements for the justification (see ECJ decision in *CHEZ Razpredelenie Bulgaria Ad v. Komisia Za Zashtita ot Diskriminatsia* [2015] IRLR 746 at [93]).

In other words, the phrase 'particular disadvantage' covers any disadvantage, and 'particular' realistically only requires that a disadvantage is identified with some accuracy as opposed to meaning that it is sufficient for a group to be broadly and non-specifically disadvantaged.

It is also not necessary to establish the reason for the particular disadvantage to which the group is put. The essential element is a causal connection between the PCP and the disadvantage suffered, not only by the group, but also by the individual (*Essop v. Home Office* [2017] IRLR 558 at [33]).

A simple approach to identifying whether there was a particular disadvantage to one group within a pool was set out in *Pendleton v. Derbyshire County Council* [2016] IRLR 580 at [38]-[44] where the employer had a policy that a refusal to end a marriage with a person convicted of making indecent images of children would be regarded as gross misconduct or some other substantial reason justifying dismissal:

> 38. Determining the question of comparative collective disadvantage is not simply answered by identifying that the PCP applies to persons both within and without the group sharing the relevant characteristic; that is simply the neutral application of the PCP. In my judgment, it is, moreover, not answered by identifying that others falling outside that group will also consider themselves disadvantaged in some way by the application of the PCP; that

again may simply be the product of the neutral application of the PCP....

...

40. First, the comparative exercise that the ET had to carry out had to be based upon groups that were – absent the particular protected characteristic – in circumstances that were the same or not materially different (s.23 EqA). That meant the comparison of both groups (those sharing the claimant's protected characteristic as compared to those who did not share that characteristic but to whom the PCP would also be applied) would involve persons who were in long-term loving relationships. If facing the very difficult personal circumstances as arose here, both groups would undoubtedly face a very real additional disadvantage if put to the election of choosing between their partner and their career. For some individuals falling into the comparator group (being in a partnership but not married or married but not sharing the same view of their marriage vows as the claimant) that disadvantage might have been the same as that suffered by the claimant. The task for the ET was, however, not to pick out particular individuals who might fall into either group but to consider the potential groups (those sharing the protected characteristic and those who did not) and ask whether – taking, as applicable to both, the difficulty inherent in such circumstances for anyone in a loving and committed relationship – those who also held a religious belief in the particular sanctity of marriage, arising from the sacrosanct nature of vows made before God, face a particular disadvantage?

...

44. ...Comparing two groups, both comprising individuals in long-term, loving and committed relationships, facing the same difficult circumstances as arose in this case and given the choice between remaining with their husband/partner or their career *but* with one group also holding a religious belief in the sanctity of their marriage vows, I conclude the ET was bound to hold that the latter had an additional burden; a particular disadvantage...

To put it another way, it must be possible to make some general statements which would be true about a group such that an employer ought reasonably to be able to appreciate that any particular provision may have a disparate adverse impact on the group (*Eweida v. British Airways plc* [2010] IRLR 322 at [24]).

How those general statements are established depends on the circumstances of a given case. Sometimes statistical evidence is relevant, sometimes expert evidence, and in some cases the tribunal can take judicial notice of a disadvantage, for instance it being generally recognised that women have more childcare responsibilities than men.

In the absence of the ability to claim combined discrimination i.e. sex and age together, it is initially difficult to envisage a PCP that puts those experiencing menopause at a disadvantage being one that in fact puts either women or those in a particular age group at that disadvantage. That is because a hypothetical group of women is likely to be made up of a range of ages including ages at which menopause is not an issue. Take, for example, a PCP requiring a certain level of performance with consequences for falling below it. That might affect an individual who is impaired by the effects of menopause, but it arguably could not be said to affect more women than men overall. Likewise, the same PCP arguably would not affect people (men and women) within a certain age group compared with people (also men and women) outside it. It is not necessarily the single protected characteristic that causes the disadvantage. On a given date (the date of application of the PCP), not all women will be experiencing menopause, and not all those in a particular age group will. A statement that a particular level of performance is not attainable could not be said generally about either sex or age, and particularly in isolation from the other.

It is not likely possible to include or exclude menopause within or from the pool for comparison. If it is correct to say that, for example, men should be impaired in the same way, then it is probably not the case that more women are affected by the example PCP relating to performance levels. If it is correct to say that men should not be impaired, that creates an artificial limitation on the pool because those men would not be affected by the PCP, meaning that the pool would be made up of all women and only unimpaired men, with the obvious result that more women than men would be affected by required performance levels. The tribunal must be careful not to create a pool to reach the conclusion that a group is disadvantaged simply because the claimant is.

This illustrates the importance of ensuring the comparison is of like-with-like. In *Cummings v. British Airways plc* [2021] IRLR 270, the respondent introduced a policy whereby one paid rest day was removed from the roster for every three unpaid parental leave days taken in a month. The claimant had two young daughters and arranged to take three days' parental leave. She was therefore rostered with one less paid rest day in that month. She claimed that the policy was indirectly discriminatory on the grounds of sex. The EAT held that the correct pool for comparison was made up of men and women where both had childcare responsibilities and the assessment had to be whether more women than men took parental leave.

In other words, both groups shared the particular condition potentially leading to the disadvantage (childcare responsibilities). In this light, it is not easy to see how a PCP is likely to affect more women than men, or women in a particular age group than others, because of the presence of menopause. It must be remembered that there is a not insignificant difference between direct and indirect discrimination. For direct discrimination, the claimant has a choice of comparator, and can ascribe (or not) individual features. In indirect discrimination cases, there is no choice. That is because indirect discrimination tests the effect of apparently neutral conditions to groups of people at large. Within those broad groups will, and must, be persons that do not share specific features with the claimant.

Indirect disability discrimination is more straightforward. The example PCP of a required performance level is more likely to affect those experiencing menopause than not. The comparator group would be persons not experiencing menopause. The test would be as to whether or not the disabled group are more disadvantaged than the non-disabled group. Subject to being able to demonstrate that, on the whole, those experiencing menopause are more likely to suffer performance issues, that disadvantage ought to be demonstrable. Of course, other PCPs are also likely to have an impact in menopause cases: attendance levels and punctuality are two obvious examples. Employers will also have PCPs applicable to their own business, and it is difficult to give an exhaustive list of requirements that could each affect employees experiencing menopause, particularly given the range of adverse effects arising therefrom.

Where there may be issues in this regard, depending on the factual circumstances, is showing that a particular PCP would have the detrimental effect on those experiencing menopause. That is because symptoms vary. It may not be readily accepted that a PCP would affect the group generally because the particular effect of menopause creating an individual disadvantage may only rarely be shared. It should not be readily assumed that there will be a group disadvantage.

However, unless the protected characteristic is the combination of sex and age, whether or not a PCP would affect those experiencing menopause, either because of sex or age, would depend a great deal on the terms of the PCP and the specific make-up of the pool of people affected by it. It is not an impossible scenario that a workplace is made up of predominately either women or people over a particular age. In that case, a PCP could well disparately affect age or sex respectively. However, that is surely a rare example.

It may be arguable that the group relied on by a claimant for comparison is made up of a combination of protected characteristics. In the case of *Ministry of Defence v. DeBique* [2010] IRLR 471, the claimant was a soldier. The respondent applied two PCPs: the first was a requirement that soldiers be available 24 hours a day, seven days a week (the '24/7 PCP'). That placed women, who were regarded as more likely to be single parents (as was the claimant), at a particular disadvantage. That PCP was justified. However, the PCP alone did not reflect the claimant's true disadvantage. The claimant's 'backup' childcare was her sister, who lived in St. Vincent. The respondent had another PCP (the 'immigration PCP') that, whilst soldiers could have another adult live with them for childcare, Foreign and Commonwealth soldiers (as was the claimant) could not invite relations from overseas. There was therefore indirect race discrimination.

The tribunal looked at the combined effect of the PCPs. It defined the pool as male and female soldiers in the British Army whose potential child carers are foreign nationals and found that women in that pool were at a particular disadvantage when compared with men. If the women in the pool were not obliged to comply with the 24/7 PCP they would not be at the disadvantage, compared with the men, caused by the immigration PCP. They would be able to use ordinary childcare arrangements. If the immigration PCP was not applied, the potential child carers of those in the pool could enter the UK and remain as carers in the long-term, avoiding the disparity between men and women in the pool. Similarly, the combined PCPs put those of Vincentian national origin at a particular disadvantage when compared with other persons in the pool. If either of the PCPs were relaxed, that disadvantage would disappear.

The EAT upheld the tribunal's decision to combine PCPs. This decision *may* increase the scope of indirect discrimination so that someone with menopause could rely on it to claim that a PCP was discriminatory as against people with the combination of age and sex. The obvious distinction between the situation in *DeBique* and what is likely to be the situation in another workplace, was that the claimant there was affected by two separate PCPs, which each impinged on one protected characteristic, rather than one PCP affecting two. It may be that there is no real practical significance in that distinction. The logic of the tribunal's rationale was that one PCP and one protected characteristic did not create the real disadvantage. The tribunal looked to that, real, disadvantage for the basis on which to assess the PCPs, and it followed that both PCPs created it. Therefore, it may follow, if someone experiencing menopause is disadvantaged because of both age and sex, but not because of one, the tribunal should look to *that* disadvantage and assess the impact of the PCP accordingly.

On the other hand, it can be said that it is very much relevant that *DeBique* involved two PCPs combined, and not one PCP affecting two characteristics. s.19 Equality Act 2010 is drafted to test the discriminatory effect of a PCP as it relates to one characteristic. The tribunal in *DeBique* did nothing different. Both PCPs were not individually discriminatory. However, the reality was that two PCPs together created a disadvantage and so the test related to their combination. That is apparent from the fact that it was stated that if one

PCP was not applied, there was no comparative disadvantage, and the same if the other was removed. That analysis does not translate to one PCP and two characteristics. The case therefore goes no further than establishing that it is possible to combine PCPs, rather than characteristics. It does not go so far as to say that one PCP can be tested against two characteristics. As above, often the PCP will dictate the pool. It was relatively straightforward to draw up a pool for comparison in *DeBique* given the presence of two PCPs i.e. it could easily be defined who was impacted by the PCP. It would conceivably be difficult to draw up a pool, in which all persons must have materially the same circumstances, but not to be artificially narrow, without creating a new protected characteristic of age/sex combined. *DeBique* does not call for that. The pool that tested both race and sex was driven by the fact of two PCPs. There was no combined characteristic as such. It could not be said that one of the PCPs affected the claimant because of her two characteristics, it was both PCPs.

There is undoubtedly argument to be had over the potential discriminatory impact of a PCP on combinations of protected characteristics, and *DeBique* is a useful starting point, but is not necessarily authoritative on the point. *DeBique* preceded the Equality Act 2010, which sought to introduce, but is yet to do so, combined direct discrimination (but not indirect discrimination). One would imagine that, if it was intended that s.19 Equality Act 2010 could accommodate more than one protected characteristic, it would have been worded accordingly.

*Individual disadvantage*

It is not enough for a claimant to establish group disadvantage. It is also not sufficient to demonstrate group disadvantage and another individual disadvantage. A claimant must also show that they have been placed at the *same* disadvantage as the group, although they do not need to show more than that.

In *Ryan v. South West Ambulance Services NHS Trust* [2021] IRLR 4, the respondent used a recruitment tool called the 'Talent Pool' to identify and develop future leaders and managers, and to retain existing leaders and managers. One of the routes into the Talent Pool was through employee appraisal. The claimant did not obtain a sufficient rating in her appraisal to gain entry to the Talent Pool. She later did not gain promotion because she was not in the Talent Pool whereas those promoted were. She claimed indirect age discrimination. There was a PCP that the respondent only promoted managerial staff on the basis of their membership of the Talent Pool. The PCP put people of the claimant's age group, namely those aged 55–70, to a particular disadvantage when compared with those who did not have that protected characteristic: that was because statistics showed that employees under age 55 had a 1/34 chance of being in the Talent Pool, whereas employees aged 55–70 had a 1/73 chance. The respondent argued that the reason the claimant did not suffer the disadvantage was not the PCP, because the claimant could not prove the causal link between the disadvantage and its stated reason for it.

The EAT confirmed the principles that claimants do not have to show the reason that a group is or would be at a disadvantage, nor the reason that the claimant is or was. A claimant only has to show a corresponding group and individual disadvantage. However, it is open to employers to show that a PCP does not in fact put the claimant at the alleged disadvantage.

*Justification*

Only if the employee proves each of (1) the existence of a PCP, (2) that it creates a disadvantage to persons sharing the particular characteristic, (3) that it creates the same disadvantage to the employee, does it fall to the employer to prove justification (*Dziedziak v. Future Electronics Ltd.* UKEAT/0271/11).

The question for the tribunal is whether or not the PCP is justified bearing in mind the fact that it places a group at a disadvantage. The above looks at whether that group disadvantage is established in a menopause case. However, a discussion on justification can only be general since it has no specific relation to any protected characteristic.

s.19(2)(d) Equality Act 2010 specifically requires both (1) the existence of a legitimate aim and (2) the proportionality of the PCP as a means of achieving it. The principles guiding this two-fold test have been set out in *MacCulloch v. ICI* [2008] IRLR 846 at [10]:

> (1) The burden of proof is on the respondent to establish justification: see *Starmer v British Airways* [2005] IRLR 862 at [31].
>
> (2) The classic test was set out in *Bilka-Kaufhaus GmbH v Weber Von Hartz* (case 170/84) [1984] IRLR 317 in the context of indirect sex discrimination. The ECJ said that the court or tribunal must be satisfied that the measures must 'correspond to a real need ... are appropriate with a view to achieving the objectives pursued and are necessary to that end' (paragraph 36). This involves the application of the proportionality principle, which is the language used in reg. 3 itself. It has subsequently been emphasised that the reference to 'necessary' means 'reasonably necessary': see *Rainey v Greater Glasgow Health Board* (HL) [1987] IRLR 26 per Lord Keith of Kinkel at pp.30–31.
>
> (3) The principle of proportionality requires an objective balance to be struck between the discriminatory effect of the measure and the needs of the undertaking. The more serious the disparate adverse impact, the more cogent must be the justification for it: *Hardy & Hansons plc v Lax* [2005] IRLR 726 per Pill LJ at paragraphs [19]–[34], Thomas LJ at [54]–[55] and Gage LJ at [60].
>
> (4) It is for the employment tribunal to weigh the reasonable needs of the undertaking against the discriminatory effect of the employer's measure and to make its own assessment of whether the former outweigh the latter. There is no 'range of reasonable response' test in this context: *Hardy & Hansons plc v Lax* [2005] IRLR 726, CA.

The elements therefore required to make out a justification defence are as follows:

1. A legitimate aim;

2. That the PCP was appropriate in order to achieve the aim;

3. That the PCP was proportionate i.e.:

    (1) It was reasonably necessary;

    (2) It struck the balance between its discriminatory effect and the aim.

A 'legitimate' aim is one that 'should be legal, should not be discriminatory in itself, and must represent a real, objective consideration' (EHRC Code at [4.28]).

The aim need not have been in the mind of the alleged discriminator at the time of applying the PCP. The tribunal must seek out the reason for the PCP, and then identify the objective being pursued. The tribunal must be satisfied that that has to be the actual objective being pursued, and it will look with care at alleged aims not in the mind of the decision-maker at the time (*Seldon v. Clarkson Wright & Jakes* [2012] IRLR 590 at [59]-[60]).

The idea of legitimate aim is undoubtedly a broad one, only realistically qualified as per the EHRC Code. However, reducing cost or preventing an increase of cost, of itself, cannot be a legitimate aim. Since the ECJ's decision in *Hill v. Revenue Commissioner* [1999] ICR 48, tribunals adopted the 'cost plus' principle, which was that cost could be used to justify an otherwise discriminatory PCP provided it was combined with other factors. That principle has been upheld most recently in *Heskett v Secretary of State for Justice* [2021] IRLR 132 at [83]-[89] (emphases added):

> 83. It follows that <u>the essential question is whether the employer's aim in acting in the way that gives rise to the discriminatory impact can fairly be described as no more than a wish to save costs. If so, the defence of justification cannot succeed.</u> But, if not, it will be necessary to arrive at a fair characterisation of the employer's aim taken as a whole and decide whether that aim is legitimate. The distinction involved may sometimes be subtle (to adopt the

> Supreme Court's language in *O'Brien*) but it is real. The nature of the distinction can be illustrated by reference to some of the cases.
>
> ...
>
> 88. ...there is certainly an established principle that, to take Rimer LJ's formulation in *Woodcock*, 'the saving or avoidance of costs will not, without more, amount to the achieving of a legitimate aim' for the purpose of the defence of justification in a discrimination claim; but that that principle needs to be understood in the way that I have sought to explain it in the preceding paragraphs. It only bites where the aim is, as the CJEU put it in *Hill and Stapleton*, 'solely' to avoid costs.
>
> 89. That being so, the 'cost plus' label (and its cognates such as 'cost alone' and 'the plus factor') cannot be said to be incorrect, and it is sometimes too convenient a shorthand to eschew. However, that language is not in fact used either by Burton P in *Cross* or by Rimer LJ in *Woodcock*, and I would prefer to avoid it so far as possible...It is better, in any case where the issue arises, to consider how the employer's aim can most fairly be characterised, looking at the total picture. It is only if the fair characterisation is indeed that the aim was solely to avoid increased costs that it has to be treated as illegitimate.

As to the proportionality of a PCP in achieving an aim, the test was summarised (and repeated) in *Homer v Chief Constable of West Yorkshire Police* [2012] ICR 704 at [20]:

> As Mummery LJ explained in *R (Elias) v Secretary of State for Defence* [2006] EWCA Civ 1293, [2006] IRLR 934, at [151]:
>
>> ... the objective of the measure in question must correspond to a real need and the means used must be appropriate with a view to achieving the objective and be necessary to that end. So it is necessary to weigh the need against the seriousness of the detriment to the disadvantaged group.

He went on, at [165], to commend the three-stage test for determining proportionality derived from *de Freitas v Permanent Secretary of Ministry of Agriculture, Fisheries, Lands and Housing* [1999] 1 AC 69, 80:

> First, is the objective sufficiently important to justify limiting a fundamental right? Secondly, is the measure rationally connected to the objective? Thirdly, are the means chosen no more than is necessary to accomplish the objective?

As the Court of Appeal held in *Hardy & Hansons plc v Lax* [2005] EWCA Civ 846, [2005] IRLR 726 [31], [32], it is not enough that a reasonable employer might think the criterion justified. The tribunal itself has to weigh the real needs of the undertaking, against the discriminatory effects of the requirement.

In order for the PCP to 'correspond to a real need', there must be 'a nexus established between the function of the employer in this type of case and the imposition of the condition otherwise it is impossible to carry out the objective balance…' (*Lea v. Greater Manchester Police Authority* [1990] IRLR 372 at [33]).

A PCP must be appropriate, or it will not be justified. For a PCP to be appropriate to achieve the real need, it should actually achieve it. The test is not subjective, and it is not sufficient for the employer to show that s/he considered his/her reasons for applying the PCP to be adequate (*Hampson v. Department of Education and Science* [1989] ICR 179).

As cited above, whether a PCP is reasonably necessary to achieve the legitimate aim is an objective assessment to be made by the tribunal, and not by reference to the reasonable employer or band of reasonable responses test (*Hardys & Hansons plc v. Lax* [2005] ICR 1565).

In determining whether or not a discriminatory PCP was reasonably necessary, the existence of non-discriminatory alternative means is a factor to take into account. However, the existence of alternative non-discriminatory means is not determinative of the question of whether or not the PCP chosen was necessary (*Kapenova v. Department of Health*

[2014] ICR 884) i.e. it does not mean that the employer was disproportionate in taking the step it did.

As to proportionality of a PCP, the tribunal should focus on the justification of the *general* rule, rather than the application in an individual case i.e. it should not consider only the impact on the claimant (*City of Oxford Bus Services Ltd. v. Harvey* UKEAT/0171/18). In the first instance, a proper analysis of the employer's needs requires 'the Tribunal to assess the reasonable needs of the business and to make its own judgment…considering whether the proposal is reasonably necessary' (*Mitchell v. David Evans Agriculture Ltd.* UKEAT/0083/06).

As regards the impact of the PCP, the tribunal must ascertain both the quantitative effect of the provision (how many people with and without the protected characteristic are affected) <u>and</u> the qualitative effect (how much damage the provision may do, how lasting the damage is, etc.) (*Jones v. University of Manchester* [1993] ICR 474). So a PCP may be justified if only a small number of, say, women are or may be affected by it, or, if the number is larger, the effect is not severe. That is an overall balancing exercise, which will undoubtedly require an employer to put forward evidence in support of its position on either or both those strands.

*Summary: indirect discrimination*

As with any discrimination claim, indirect discrimination is highly fact-sensitive. An employer can set down any number and variation of rule or requirement, and it is not possible to imagine all or any of them here. However, the principal question will be whether or not a PCP puts women or those of a certain age group at a disadvantage. For a claimant to succeed, they must consider what the disadvantage is, and why it is caused, then work out why it could be said that the same disadvantage would be caused to women and/or a particular age group. From there, it should be possible to craft the wording of the PCP.

There is no doubt that indirect discrimination claims are difficult in general, and more so in the case of application to menopause cases.

There may be less difficulty in disability cases, but the above hurdles remain to be overcome, not least in showing group disadvantage.

Of course, a PCP could be justified. If a small number of people are disadvantaged and/or not greatly, it may well be proportionate to apply it.

Overall, a claimant must think carefully before pleading indirect discrimination, and must make sure all the requirements of s.19 Equality Act 2010 are met. It is unhelpful to plead a claim of indirect discrimination in a broad manner, with assumptions around group disadvantage and identification of PCPs. Specificity is crucial.

## Harassment

When one considers the word 'harassment', the image of repetitive grinding down of an individual comes to mind. In fact, harassment under the Equality Act 2010, whilst including that form of conduct, is much wider. It is necessary, of course, that the conduct has grounding in a protected characteristic, and there is no protection from general offence. For harassment to occur under the Equality Act 2010, conduct must relate to a protected characteristic. It is not only where conduct is because of the characteristic that it might be unlawful. This therefore proscribes a much wider field of behaviour. Comments or actions done because of menopause, ought, as set out below, be capable of relating to sex, age, or disability since menopause itself does.

As with all protective provisions, s.26 Equality Act 2010 (harassment) includes a number of hurdles that must be overcome before a claim under it is successful, each of which is explored below.

s.26 Equality Act 2010 provides:

> (1) A person (A) harasses another (B) if—
>
> > (a) A engages in unwanted conduct related to a relevant protected characteristic, and
> >
> > (b) the conduct has the purpose or effect of—

(i) violating B's dignity, or

(ii) creating an intimidating, hostile, degrading, humiliating or offensive environment for B.

...

(3) A also harasses B if—

(a) A or another person engages in unwanted conduct of a sexual nature or that is related to gender reassignment or sex,

(b) the conduct has the purpose or effect referred to in subsection (1)(b), and

(c) because of B's rejection of or submission to the conduct, A treats B less favourably than A would treat B if B had not rejected or submitted to the conduct.

(4) In deciding whether conduct has the effect referred to in subsection (1)(b), each of the following must be taken into account—

(a) the perception of B;

(b) the other circumstances of the case;

(c) whether it is reasonable for the conduct to have that effect.

(5) The relevant protected characteristics are—

- age;
- disability;
- gender reassignment;
- race;

- religion or belief;
- sex;
- sexual orientation.

It is entirely possible for conduct towards an employee in relation to menopause to, on the face of it, amount to harassment. However, one must consider the component parts of s.26 Equality Act 2010 before harassment concluding that is established.

*Unwanted conduct*

The basis of harassment is that it undermines an employee's dignity. It follows that the conduct must be unwanted. 'Unwanted conduct' is an essential ingredient in establishing harassment.

What conduct is capable of amounting to harassment is apparently limitless. The EHRC Code lists, by way of example, at para. 7.7 'spoken or written words or abuse, imagery, graffiti, physical gestures, facial expressions, mimicry, jokes, pranks, acts affecting a person's surroundings or other physical behaviour'.

Spreading rumours about an employee's menopause is likely to constitute unwanted conduct (see *Nixon v. Ross Coates Solicitors* UKEAT/0108/10 in relation to gossip about an employee's pregnancy).

Revealing that another employee is menopausal may also possibly amount to unwanted conduct (see *HM Land Registry v. Grant* [2011] ICR 1390 to the opposite effect – that an employee putting information about themselves into the public domain takes the risk that s/he would become the subject of gossip).

Suspension may amount to unwanted conduct and therefore harassment (*Prospects for People with Learning Disabilities v. Harris* UKEAT/0612/11).

Express dismissal can be unwanted conduct for the purposes of s.26 Equality Act 2010 (*Urso v. Department for Work & Pensions* [2017] IRLR 304).

A constructive dismissal can amount to unwanted conduct (and harassment) so that earlier acts that contribute to a breach of contract can, individually be acts of harassment, and, in effect, the resignation in response to the breach of contract (which, of course, is termination of contract in circumstances in which the employee is entitled to terminate) can also be an act of harassment (see *Driscoll v. V&P Global Ltd.* UKEAT/0010/21 disagreeing with *Timothy James Consulting Ltd. v. Wilton* [2015] ICR 764).

Whether conduct is unwanted is a question of fact. The EHRC Code sets out at para. 7.8 that 'unwanted' simply means 'unwelcome' or 'uninvited'. The conduct must be unwanted by the recipient (*Thomas Sanderson Blinds Ltd. v. English* UKEAT/0316/10) rather than in some general sense of the conduct being unacceptable. The tribunal must therefore assess the employee's subjective perception of the conduct.

That is also apparent from the EAT's guidance on unwanted conduct in *Reed v. Bull Systems Ltd.* [1999] IRLR 299 at [27]:

> The essential characteristic of sexual harassment is that it is words or conduct which are unwelcome to the recipient and it is for the recipient to decide for themselves what is acceptable to them and what they regard as offensive...Because it is for each individual to determine what they find unwelcome or offensive, there may be cases where there is a gap between what a tribunal would regard as acceptable and what the individual in question was prepared to tolerate. It does not follow that because the tribunal would not have regarded the acts complained of as unacceptable, the complaint must be dismissed.

Some conduct could not properly be said to be welcome – it will be self-evidently unwelcome and will automatically be regarded as such. At the other end of the scale, someone may appear unduly sensitive, but, since s/he is the one to determine whether conduct was unwelcome, that should be made clear so that any reasonable employer could understand that there was an objection (see *Reed*). The absence of any objection might well (but not necessarily will) mean, in the latter scenario, that the conduct will be taken by a tribunal not to be unwanted. Even in the former scenario, if there is 'clearly' no objection through words or conduct to what would otherwise automatically be regarded as unwanted conduct, it will not be regarded as such.

What is a 'clear' lack of objection is not necessarily simple to come by, and it is difficult to imagine that a tribunal will readily accept that conduct was 'clearly' invited or welcome without particularly strong evidence. It is often thought that the alleged victim's participation in joking or banter, even about their own characteristic or condition, will amount to a lack of objection and therefore undermine the notion that conduct on the part of the alleged harasser was unwelcome. That can be true, and one could imagine someone experiencing menopause perhaps making light of some symptoms.

That, however, is not a green light for colleagues to assume that 'anything goes'. Such an issue came up in *Smith v. Ideal Shopping Direct Ltd.* UKEAT/0590/12. Although the claimant, who was openly gay, had taken part in some homophobic language, it was held that that did not mean he agreed to all conduct, particularly conduct that went beyond that to which he had already consented. It was stated thus: 'We quite accept that a person who parades their particular characteristic loudly and vocally might expect to receive from colleagues' responses or comments which make reference to that sexuality. But that is quite different from the 'abusive' use of references to sexual orientation or any other protected characteristic' (although see *Evans v. Xactly Corporation Ltd.* UKEAT/0129/18 for an example of a case in which the claimant was 'an active participant in inappropriate comments and behaviour in the workplace and seemingly comfortable with the office culture and environment' in which case there was no unwanted conduct).

Care should also be exercised where conduct has continued without *specific* objection. It should not be assumed, in those circumstances, that the absence of an express objection in fact amounts to a subjective lack of objection, clear or otherwise. For example, in *Munchkins Restaurant Ltd. v. Karmazyn and others* UKEAT/0359/09, where the employees remained in employment for some not insignificant periods, they were not taken to have invited the conduct of the employer. This is because the employees had found a way of tackling the conduct and had managed to find 'an equilibrium at work which made the job acceptable'. It was said that 'there are many situations in life where people will put up with unwanted or even criminal conduct which violates their personal dignity because they are constrained by social circumstances to do so…Putting up with it does not make it welcome, or less criminal. It is therefore not completely beyond the scope of reason to think that women in this particular situation should behave as they did'.

*Related to relevant protected characteristic*

The phrase 'related to' is plainly wider than 'because of' or 'on the grounds of'. There is no need, in the former case, for a causative link between the conduct and the protected characteristic. There is only a need for a connection or association between the two, and conduct that cannot be said to be because of a protected characteristic can still be related to it.

The test of 'related to' is an objective one to be applied by the tribunal. Determination of the relationship between conduct and characteristic is one that takes into account all the facts, including the intention of the alleged harasser, albeit that is not determinative. Likewise, the perception of the alleged victim of the relationship between conduct and characteristic is relevant but not determinative. As the EAT put it in *Bakkali v. Greater Manchester Bus (South) Ltd.* [2018] ICR 1481 at [31]:

> 'related to' 'includes a wider category of conduct. A decision on whether conduct is related to such a characteristic requires a broader inquiry…[it] requires a more intense focus on the context of the offending words or behaviour…'the mental processes' of the alleged harasser will be relevant to the question of whether the conduct complained of was related to a protected characteristic of the claimant…such evidence from the alleged perpetrator is not essential to the determination of the issue. A tribunal will determine the complaint on the material before it including evidence of the context in which the conduct complained of took place.

The EAT there emphasised the need for the tribunal to consider the overall picture, a requirement set out, also by the EAT, in *Hartley v. Foreign and Commonwealth Office Services* [2016] ICR D17 where the tribunal incorrectly focused on the alleged harassers' perception of their comments rather than looking at 'the picture in the round' and asking whether the comments related to the claimant's disability (Asperger's syndrome).

Depending on the contexts and facts of an individual case, where there is conduct directed at menopause, whether that be in general or towards an employee that is experiencing menopause at the time, that will surely be conduct that relates to sex, age, and disability (if applicable). Certainly, in the tribunal's decision in *A v. Bonmarche Ltd.*, case number 4107766/2019, conduct towards the claimant that included comments referring to her as 'a dinosaur', criticism of her for failing to staple together two pieces of paper and relating it to being menopausal, and other numerous comments relating to the claimant being menopausal, were found with 'absolutely no doubt' to be harassment. The conduct, it was said, related to the claimant's status as a woman experiencing menopause, and, as such, was related to age and sex.

It must, however, be remembered that a claimant must still prove the relationship between their protected characteristic, or between their menopause, and the conduct complained of. In some cases, it will be obvious. In others, it might not be. A claimant must therefore be prepared to show facts from which it could be concluded that conduct had some association with their menopause or effects of it. For instance, someone dismissed for alleged misconduct, which on its face has nothing to do with menopause, must show that menopause could in fact be the real reason for dismissal. That will be a matter of proving primary facts that in turn create the required inference. It will not be sufficient to point to a protected characteristic, the conduct, and the fact that the conduct was unwanted must be established.

*Effect*

Harassment will be unlawful if it has *either* the purpose *or* effect of violating an employee's dignity etc. A claim based on purpose requires analysis of the alleged harasser's thought-processes, but a claim based on effect renders those thought-processes irrelevant (and means that that claim is generally easier to prove).

Note that it is not enough for the unwanted conduct to be merely intimidating, hostile, degrading, humiliating or offensive. Rather, the conduct must create such an 'environment'. An 'environment' is a state of affairs, which must be considered in the context of the workplace in general. Whether the requisite environment had been created (which itself connotes a new state of affairs), depends on all the factors applicable in the individual case. So, in *Weeks v. Newham College of Further Education* UKEAT/0630/11, where the EAT stated at [21] 'An environment…may be created by an incident, but the effects are of longer duration. Words spoken must be seen in context; that context includes other words spoken and the general run of affairs within the office or staff-room concerned. We cannot say that the frequency of use of such words is irrelevant'. It went on to hold that the factors taken into account by the tribunal, namely that the conduct was not aimed towards the claimant, the fact that she made no complaint at the time, and the fact that the words used were only occasional, were legitimate factors to consider when determining the question of environment.

It should also be borne in mind that 'Dignity is not necessarily violated by things said or done which are trivial or transitory, particularly if it should have been clear that any offence was unintended. While it is very important that employers, and tribunals, are sensitive to the hurt that can be caused by racially offensive comments or conduct (or indeed comments or conduct on other grounds covered by the cognate legislation to which we have referred), it is also important not to encourage a culture of hypersensitivity or the imposition of legal liability in respect of every unfortunate phrase' (*Richmond Pharmacology v. Dhaliwal* [2009] ICR 724 at [27]).

The assessment of whether conduct has the effect of amounting to harassment is an objective one taking into account all the facts, but the claimant's subjective perception must also be considered, along with the understanding, motive and intention of the alleged harasser (*Driskel v. Peninsula Business Services Ltd.* [2000] IRLR 151). Those considerations are now set out in s.26(4) Equality Act 2010, the subjective element being the perception of the employee, and the objective element being the reasonableness of that perception.

In *Pemberton v. Inwood* [2018] ICR 1291 at [88], Underhill LJ set out the following approach to the consideration of whether or not unwanted conduct had the proscribed effect:

> ...a tribunal must consider *both* ...whether the putative victim perceives themselves to have suffered the effect in question (the subjective question) *and*...whether it was reasonable for the conduct to be regarded as having that effect (the objective question). It must also, of course, take into account all the other circumstances...

The relevance of those elements was set out by Underhill LJ as follows (also at [88]): 'The relevance of the subjective question is that if the claimant does not perceive their dignity to have been violated, or an adverse environment created, then the conduct should not be found to have had that effect. The relevance of the objective question is that if it was not reasonable for the conduct to be regarded as violating the claimant's dignity or creating an adverse environment for him or her, then it should not be found to have done so'.

The fact that the tribunal should consider the 'other circumstances' of the case should not be overlooked. The EHRC Code at [7.18(b)] suggests that some circumstances could be 'personal circumstances of the worker experiencing the conduct; for example, the worker's health, including mental health; mental capacity; cultural norms; or previous experience of harassment; and also the environment in which the conduct takes place'. Reference to the employee's health is likely to be particularly significant in the case of someone experiencing menopause – the fact of enduring various symptoms and that being compounded by a colleague's or employer's conduct will probably lean a tribunal towards a finding of harassment.

*Summary: harassment*

Undoubtedly, harassment under s.26 Equality Act 2010 is a much bigger 'target' than direct discrimination for those seeking to make a claim based on unwelcome conduct where a protected characteristic is involved. Consider the requirements 'detriment' and 'less favourable' compared with 'unwanted conduct', and compare 'because of' with 'related to'.

Provided an employer's conduct has the requisite effect (which is not a requirement of s.13 Equality Act 2010), a claim under s.26 Equality Act 2010, where there is no comparator required, is ostensibly much more likely to succeed. However, a claimant must still satisfy the burden of proving that a protected characteristic played a part in the conduct, so success is not a given.

As with any claim, serious thought must be given to each of the requirements of s.26 Equality Act 2010, and a claimant must be prepared to explain, other than in obvious cases, why their protected characteristic was a feature of the behaviour in question, and why it would be reasonable to regard that behaviour as violating their dignity etc. It will not be sufficient to make bald statements, and it will be helpful to all concerned to identify the factual issues at an early stage.

# CHAPTER FIVE

# DISCRIMINATION SPECIFICALLY IN RELATION TO DISABLED PERSONS

## Discrimination arising from disability

The Equality Act 2010 provides additional protection for disabled people. Whilst other protected characteristics have protection confined to direct and indirect discrimination, and harassment, there are two further provisions applicable to disabled people, the first being that set out in s.15 Equality Act 2010: discrimination because of something arising in consequence of disability.

The protection provided, whilst a form of direct discrimination in that it requires a claimant to identify a particular mindset of the employer i.e. a reason for acting, that reason/mindset need not be the disability itself, but is instead one (or more) step(s) removed from the disability. That protects disabled people from unfavourable treatment (not less favourable than a comparator) based on the effects of their disability. Therefore, if menopause amounts to a disability in a given case, there will be a viable claim where a reason for treatment is some consequence of that, for example poor performance, conduct, attendance.

The balance to that wider protection is that an employer may justify its treatment.

s.15 Equality Act 2010 provides:

(1) A person (A) discriminates against a disabled person (B) if—

(a) A treats B unfavourably because of something arising in consequence of B's disability, and

(b) A cannot show that the treatment is a proportionate means of achieving a legitimate aim.

(2) Subsection (1) does not apply if A shows that A did not know, and could not reasonably have been expected to know, that B had the disability.

*Unfavourable treatment*

There is no definition of 'unfavourable' treatment. The EHRC Code at [5.7] refers to the employee being put at a disadvantage. That, on its face, brings the concept in line with that of 'detriment' in s.39 Equality Act 2010. However, the section is deliberately drafted not to use the term 'detriment' and so, presumably, 'unfavourable' and 'detriment' must be taken to be different.

The matter was addressed in *Trustees of Swansea University Pension and Assurance Scheme v. Williams* [2019] ICR 230. The issue in the case was that the claimant had made an application for ill-health retirement, which was successful, and which entitled him to a final salary pension. However, by the time of his retirement, the claimant had reduced his hours to cope with his disabilities, which in turn reduced his salary. His pension was therefore calculated by reference to the lower salary. He claimed that that calculation, which was a term of the scheme, was unfavourable treatment.

One can see that that could amount to a detriment. However, Langstaff J in the EAT concluded that 'unfavourable' could not be equated with 'detriment', and that 'unfavourable' when used elsewhere in the Equality Act 2010 'had the sense of 'placing a hurdle in front of, or creating a particular difficulty for, or disadvantaging a person …". Subjecting someone to a detriment is not necessarily the same thing. In fact, in the particular case, Langstaff J concluded that treatment that confers an advantage (the ill-health pension) is not unfavourable merely because it is 'insufficiently advantageous'. Whether, technically, the calculation based on the lower salary was detrimental or not, it was not <u>un</u>favourable. Unfavourable is to be measured 'against an objective sense of that which is adverse as compared with that which is beneficial'.

In the Supreme Court judgment, Lord Carnwath stated at [27] 'in most cases (including the present) little is likely to be gained by seeking to draw narrow distinctions between the word 'unfavourably' in section 15 and analogous concepts such as 'disadvantage' or 'detriment' found in other provisions, nor between an objective and a 'subjective/objective' approach. While the passages in the [EHRC Code]...cannot replace the statutory words, they do in my view provide helpful advice as to the relatively low threshold of disadvantage which is sufficient to trigger the requirement to justify under this section'. In other words, it might be appropriate to consider whether an employee has been subjected to a detriment in order to determine whether there has been unfavourable treatment, but caution should be exercised, and one must remember the difference between the concepts since, in a marginal case, it could make the difference, as in *Williams*.

*Because of something arising in consequence of disability*

The 'because of something arising in consequence of disability' is a two-stage test: (1) what was the reason for unfavourable treatment (the 'something'); and (2) did that arise in consequence of disability, although the tribunal may ask those questions in either order (see *Basildon and Thurrock NHS Foundation Trust v. Weerasinghe* [2016] ICR 305).

The EAT in *Pnaiser v. NHS England* [2016] IRLR 170 at [31] summarised the 'proper approach' to s.15 Equality Act 2010 in the following terms (emphases added):

(a) A Tribunal must first identify whether there was unfavourable treatment and by whom: in other words, it must ask whether A treated B unfavourably in the respects relied on by B. No question of comparison arises.

(b) The Tribunal must determine what caused the impugned treatment, or what was the reason for it. The focus at this stage is on the reason in the mind of A. An examination of the conscious or unconscious thought processes of A is likely to be required, just as it is in a direct discrimination case. Again, just as there may be more than one reason or cause for impugned treatment in a direct discrimination context, so too, there may be more than one reason in a section 15 case. <u>The 'something' that causes the unfavourable treatment need not be the main or sole reason, but must have at least a</u>

significant (or more than trivial) influence on the unfavourable treatment, and so amount to an effective reason for or cause of it.

(c) Motives are irrelevant. The focus of this part of the enquiry is on the reason or cause of the impugned treatment and A's motive in acting as he or she did is simply irrelevant: see *Nagarajan v London Regional Transport* [1999] IRLR 572. A discriminatory motive is emphatically not (and never has been) a core consideration before any prima facie case of discrimination arises…

(d) The Tribunal must determine whether the reason/cause (or, if more than one), a reason or cause, is 'something arising in consequence of B's disability'. That expression 'arising in consequence of' could describe a range of causal links. Having regard to the legislative history of section 15 of the Act (described comprehensively by Elisabeth Laing J in *Hall* [*v. Chief Constable of West Yorkshire Police* [2015] IRLR 893]), the statutory purpose which appears from the wording of section 15, namely to provide protection in cases where the consequence or effects of a disability lead to unfavourable treatment, and the availability of a justification defence, the causal link between the something that causes unfavourable treatment and the disability may include more than one link. In other words, more than one relevant consequence of the disability may require consideration, and it will be a question of fact assessed robustly in each case whether something can properly be said to arise in consequence of disability.

(e) For example, in *Land Registry v Houghton* UKEAT/0149/14 a bonus payment was refused by A because B had a warning. The warning was given for absence by a different manager. The absence arose from disability. The Tribunal and HHJ Clark in the EAT had no difficulty in concluding that the statutory test was met. However, the more links in the chain there are between the disability and the reason for the impugned treatment, the harder it is likely to be to establish the requisite connection as a matter of fact.

(f) This stage of the causation test involves an objective question and does not depend on the thought processes of the alleged discriminator.

(g) [As to whether] the alleged discriminator must know that the 'something' that causes the treatment arises in consequence of disability... paragraphs 26 to 34 of *Weerasinghe*...do not support [the submission that they must know], and indeed paragraph 34 highlights the difference between the two stages – the 'because of' stage involving A's explanation for the treatment (and conscious or unconscious reasons for it) and the 'something arising in consequence' stage involving consideration of whether (as a matter of fact rather than belief) the 'something' was a consequence of the disability.

(h) Moreover, the statutory language of section 15(2) makes clear...that the knowledge required is of the disability only, and does not extend to a requirement of knowledge that the 'something' leading to the unfavourable treatment is a consequence of the disability. Had this been required the statute would have said so. Moreover, the effect of section 15 would be substantially restricted...and there would be little or no difference between a direct disability discrimination claim under section 13 and a discrimination arising from disability claim under section 15.

Confirmation that there is no room in s.15 Equality Act 2010 to require that the alleged discriminator must know of the connection between the 'something' causing unfavourable treatment and the disability followed in *City of York Council v. Grossett* [2018] EWCA Civ 1105. There, a teacher showed an 18-rated film to 15-16-year-olds. He was dismissed for gross misconduct. However, he had been under stress as a result of his disability, cystic fibrosis, and had more difficulty in adapting to an increased workload. Showing the film was an error of judgment as the result of his stress, which in large part arose from his disability. The Court of Appeal noted the two-stage test above, identifying them as 'an investigation of two distinctive causative issues', but stating at [39] that 'it is not possible to spell out of s.15(1)(a) a further requirement, that A must be shown to have been aware when choosing to subject B to the unfavourable treatment in question that the relevant 'something' arose in consequence of B's disability (i.e. that A should himself be aware of the objective causation referred to in issue (ii) [whether the something arose in consequence of disability] above). That argument was not compatible with the terms of s 15, read as a whole'.

Whether the reason for treatment arises in consequence of disability is to be considered broadly. So, in *Risby v. London Borough of Waltham Forest* UKEAT/0318/15, where the claimant had a short temper, which was not related to his disability (paraplegia), but which resulted in him shouting at colleagues and managers and using racist terms, he benefitted from protection under s.15 Equality Act 2010. The reason was that, although there was no direct connection between the loss of temper and disability, the shouting was the result of the employer's decision to change the venue of a workshop to one without wheelchair access, and therefore not accessible to the claimant. The EAT stated at [18] that 'If he had not been disabled by paraplegia, he would not have been angered by the Respondent's decision to hold the first workshop in a venue to which he could not gain access. His misconduct was the product of indignation caused by that decision. His disability was an effective cause of that indignation and so of his conduct'.

That significantly broadens protection under s.15 Equality Act 2010 in that the disability need only be an effective cause of the 'something', and the 'something' need only be an effective cause of the unfavourable treatment. However, the test is not infinitely broad. There is a difference between the disability providing cause and it providing context. In *Charlesworth v. Dransfields Engineering Ltd.* UKEAT/0197/16, when the claimant was absent for cancer treatment, the respondent recognised that there was no longer a requirement for employees to do the kind of work being done by him, i.e. that of branch manager. He was therefore redundant, but that decision was not discrimination because of something arising in consequence of disability because the absence itself was not the influence or cause operating on the mind of the employer. There was a link between disability and dismissal, but only in the sense that the absence showed the respondent that there was no need for someone to work in the claimant's role.

There may also be cases in which it can be said that there is no connection between disability and the reason for treatment or that the connection is too tenuous. In *iForce Ltd. v. Wood* UKEAT/0167/18, the claimant refused to work near loading doors because she believed the conditions there were colder and would make her osteoarthritis worse. She was given a final written warning. That was not discrimination because, although the connection between disability and the reason for treatment may involve several links (rather than be the immediate cause), her *belief* that her condition would be worse by the loading doors was not correct. That area was no colder than other areas in which she worked. Her disability did not cause her belief to be wrong, and therefore, it could not be said that her refusal to work by loading doors (based on an erroneous belief) was caused by disability.

In the case of someone whose work is suffering as a result of menopausal symptoms (and who is disabled as a result of that condition), s.15 Equality Act 2010 is a helpful provision. The effects of menopause that are apt for protection under s.15 Equality Act 2010 are wide. The EHRC Code at [5.9] provides that 'The consequences of a disability include anything which is the result, effect or outcome of a disabled person's disability. The consequences will be varied, and will depend on the individual effect upon a disabled person of their disability. Some consequences may be obvious, such as an inability to walk unaided or inability to use certain work equipment. Others may not be obvious, for example, having to follow a restricted diet' (emphasis added). So, where work performance has dipped or perhaps misconduct has been committed, and even where the employer does not know why, but places the employee at a detriment nevertheless, the employee is likely protected by s.15 Equality Act 2010, subject to the employer's justification of the treatment.

For example, in *Davies v. Scottish Courts and Tribunals Service*, case number 4104575/2017, the claimant, who was a court officer, suffered a range of adverse effects of menopause (and was disabled) including stress, anxiety, and memory loss. She became concerned when she saw two men drinking water that had been on her desk in the court. Her concern was that she could not recall whether or not she had poured her medication into that water. She approached the men, who later reported that she had raised her voice, and informed them that her medication may be in the water. She was dismissed for, amongst other things, failing to manage her medication sufficiently so that she misled the individuals into believing they had ingested medication, and did so by shouting at them. The tribunal found that the Claimant's conduct was 'affected by her disability insofar as her condition caused her to be confused and forgetful about whether she had taken her medication and whether she had put it in the water jug…It also caused her to be anxious and to react to the situation by raising her voice'. The tribunal was satisfied that there was a causal link between disability and conduct.

*Knowledge*

There can be no discrimination under s.15 Equality Act 2010 unless the employer knows or could reasonably have known that the employee has the disability. That therefore poses a potential difficulty for an individual that wishes to 'suffer in silence', and not inform their employer about their menopause and its effects. That does not entitle the employer to disregard evidence that might point to menopause (or any disability). They should consider whether a disability might be behind performance, conduct, or other concerns, as the case may be. The EHRC Code states at [5.14]: 'Employers should consider whether a worker has a disability even where one has not been formally disclosed, as, for example, not all workers who meet the definition of disability may think of themselves as a 'disabled person'', and at [5.15] 'An employer must do all they can reasonably be expected to do to find out if a worker has a disability. What is reasonable will depend on the circumstances. This is an objective assessment. When making enquiries about disability, employers should consider issues of dignity and privacy and ensure that personal information is dealt with confidentially', with the final sentence being particularly important in sensitive cases.

The EAT summarised the principles in relation to knowledge in *A Ltd. v. Z* [2019] IRLR 952 at [23] as follows:

(1) There need only be actual or constructive knowledge as to the disability itself, not the causal link between the disability and its consequent effects which led to the unfavourable treatment, see *City of York Council v Grosset* [2018] EWCA

Civ 1105, [2018] IRLR 746, [2018] ICR 1492 CA at para 39.

(2) The Respondent need not have constructive knowledge of the complainant's diagnosis to satisfy the requirements of s 15(2); it is, however, for the employer to show that it was unreasonable for it to be expected to know that a person (a) suffered an impediment to his physical or mental health, or (b) that that impairment had a substantial and (c) long-term effect, see *Donelien v Liberata UK Ltd* (2014) UKEAT/0297/14, [2014] All ER (D) 253 (Dec) at para 5, per Langstaff P, and also see *Pnaiser v NHS England* (2016) UKEAT/0137/15/LA, [2016] IRLR 170 EAT at para 69 per Simler J.

(3) The question of reasonableness is one of fact and evaluation, see [2018] EWCA Civ 129, [2018] IRLR 535 CA at para [27]; nonetheless, such assessments must be adequately and coherently reasoned and must take into account all relevant factors and not take into account those that are irrelevant.

(4) When assessing the question of constructive knowledge, an employee's representations as to the cause of absence or disability related symptoms can be of importance: (i) because, in asking whether the employee has suffered substantial adverse effect, a reaction to life events may fall short of the definition of disability for EqA purposes (see *Herry v Dudley Metropolitan Council* (2016) UKEAT/0100/16, [2017] ICR 610, per His Honour Judge Richardson, citing *J v DLA Piper UK LLP* (2010) UKEAT/0263/09, [2010] IRLR936, [2010] ICR 1052), and (ii) because, without knowing the likely cause of a given impairment, '*it becomes much more difficult to know whether it may well last for more than 12 months, if it is not* [*already done so*]', per Langstaff P in *Donelien* EAT at para 31.

(5) The approach adopted to answering the question thus posed by s 15(2) is to be informed by the Code, which (relevantly) provides [[5.14] and [5.15] as set out above]

(6) It is not incumbent upon an employer to make every enquiry where there is little or no basis for doing so (*Ridout v T C Group* (1998) EAT/137/97, [1998] IRLR 628; *Alam v Secretary of State for the Department for Work and Pensions* (2009) UKEAT/0242/09, [2010] IRLR 283, [2010] ICR 665).

(7) Reasonableness, for the purposes of s 15(2), must entail a balance between the strictures of making enquiries, the likelihood of such enquiries yielding results and the dignity and privacy of the employee, as recognised by the Code.

So, if an employer suspects that a woman within a relevant age group is suffering from adverse effects of menopause, it would be wise to at least ask the employee about the cause of her work issues without necessarily suggesting the underlying cause. From there, it could consider the likelihood of disability in the sense of the level of effect and potential timeframe. As above, the employer need not know, actually or constructively, that the employee specifically is experiencing menopause. In *Urso v. Department of Work and Pensions* [2017] IRLR 304, the EAT stated at [40] that the employer is 'required to consider the symptoms and effect of the Claimant's disability…There may well be cases where the specific cause of the disability is not known or has not been identified at the material time. What is important is that the employer consider the effect of the impairment'.

Any such enquiry must be handled with tact. In the case of *Best v. Embark on Raw Ltd., case number 3202006/2020*, an employee that had made it clear with a customer that she did not wish to discuss her possible menopause, was harassed within the meaning of s.26 Equality Act 2010 when a director, who had seen her conversation with the customer, 'pursued' the topic, and 'tactlessly' asked her directly whether she was menopausal. The tribunal found that that conduct violated her dignity and created a humiliating environment for her.

The question of whether the employer could reasonably be expected to know of the disability is not the same as whether they could reasonably have enquired. The tribunal must go further and also consider what the enquiry would yield. In *A Ltd. v. Z*, the employer could not have had constructive knowledge where the employee would have suppressed information about her mental health (had the employer carried out a reasonable enquiry). That is a matter that will be relevant in cases involving menopause, as with many disabilities, because it may be that an employee would rather not provide much or any information to their employer. Each case will be different. Even if an employer does enquire but is not sufficiently informed, or indeed where the employee specifically denies the possibility of any disability, that employer may be entitled not to press further (see *Ridout v. TC Group* [1998] IRLR 628 where it was said that 'people must be taken very much on the basis of how they present themselves').

However, an employer must not simply 'rubber-stamp' advice of occupational health without further consideration, or without applying their own judgment (*Gallop v. Newport City Council* [2013] EWCA Civ 1583).

Finally, the EHRC Code states at [5.17] that knowledge gained by people working for the employer (with the exception of those providing services to workers independently of the employer (see [5.19]) will be imputed to the employer:

> If an employer's agent or employee (such as an occupational health adviser or a HR officer) knows, in that capacity, of a worker's or applicant's or potential applicant's disability, the employer will not usually be able to claim that they do not know of the disability, and that they cannot therefore have subjected a disabled person to discrimination arising from disability.

*Justification and interaction with other provisions*

The justification test in s.15 Equality Act 2010 is naturally similar to that of the test under s.19 Equality Act 2010. Therefore, much of what is said in the chapter on indirect discrimination applies here. However, that chapter is not directly transferable into this. As the EAT cautioned in *Stott v. Ralli Ltd.* UKEAT/0223/20 (at [81]), it must be remembered that, in each provision, the employer is seeking to justify a different thing (PCP giving rise to group disadvantage in one, treatment of an individual in another). The quantitative discriminatory impact need not therefore be considered.

The law on justification under s.15 Equality Act 2010 was summarised in *Ali v. Torrosian* UKEAT/0029/18 at [15]-[20] as follows:

> 15. …To be proportionate, the conduct in question has to be both an appropriate means of achieving a legitimate aim and a reasonably necessary means of doing so…
>
> 16. Justification of the unfavourable treatment requires there to be an objective balance between the discriminatory effect and the reasonable needs of the employer…
>
> 17. …when determining whether or not a measure is proportionate it will be relevant for the ET to consider whether or not any lesser measure might nevertheless have served the employer's legitimate aim…
>
> 18. More specifically, the case law acknowledges that it will be for the ET to undertake a fair and detailed assessment of the working practices and business considerations involved, and to have regard to the business needs of the employer…In that context, the severity of the impact on the employer of the continuing absence of an employee who is on long-term sickness absence will, no doubt, be a significant element in the balance that will determine the point at which their dismissal becomes justified, albeit, the evidence that may be required in this respect will be primarily a matter for the ET…
>
> 19. …As Underhill LJ acknowledged in *O'Brien*, in carrying out the assessment required for the purposes of section 15 EqA , the ET is applying a different legal test to that arising in the context of an unfair dismissal claim under section 98 ERA. That said, Underhill LJ went on to deprecate the introduction of additional complexity where the substantive assessment is likely to be the same. Specifically, as he identified, where an ET is concerned with both such claims in the context of a dismissal for long-term sickness absence, the factors that are relevant for its determination of one

> claim are likely to be substantially the same as those to be weighed in the other (see paragraphs 53 to 55 of *O'Brien*).
>
> 20. As to the time at which justification needs to be established, that is when the unfavourable treatment in question is applied...When the putative discriminator has not even considered questions of proportionality at that time, it is likely to be more difficult for them to establish justification...

The focus on individual treatment, and whether it was reasonably necessary to achieve a legitimate aim, brings with a consideration of whether or not the employer could make reasonable adjustments (considered in the following chapter) to mitigate the treatment, or avoid it altogether. Any failure to comply with the duty to make adjustments is simply part of the balancing exercise of justification. However, it is difficult to see how unfavourable treatment, that could have been avoided by making reasonable adjustments, could also be justified – see *Dominique v. Toll Global Forwarding Ltd.* UKEAT/0308/13 and the following comments of Elias LJ in *Griffiths v. Department of Work and Pensions* [2017] ICR 760 at [26]:

> An employer who dismisses a disabled employee without making a reasonable adjustment which would have enabled the employee to remain in employment — say allowing him to work part-time — will necessarily have infringed the duty to make adjustments, but in addition the act of dismissal will surely constitute an act of discrimination arising out of disability. The dismissal will be for a reason related to disability and if a potentially reasonable adjustment which might have allowed the employee to remain in employment has not been made, the dismissal will not be justified.

However, not making adjustments at some point earlier than the time of the unfavourable treatment is not necessarily fatal to a justification defence (see e.g. *Monmouthshire County Council v. Harris* UKEAT/0332/14).

Many cases will involve both unfair dismissal and discrimination arising from disability. There are two different tests (unfair dismissal is considered in more detail in later chapters). It was thought at one point (referred to in *Torrosian* above) that there was sufficient similarity between the band of reasonable responses test and the justification test that the former followed the latter (following *O'Brien v. Bolton St. Catherine's Academy* [2017] EWCA Civ 145). However, that is not the proper approach to those two different tests, which are described as plainly distinct (*City of York Council v. Grossett* [2018] EWCA Civ 1105 at [55]). One (unfair dismissal) looks at procedural considerations, the other (discrimination) is purely objective with no room for looking at the actions and thought-processes of the employer (*Department of Work and Pensions v. Boyers* UKEAT/0282/19 at [38]). They must be assessed separately.

There is also, finally, a potential overlap with indirect discrimination. That was set out in *Griffiths v. Department of Work and Pensions* [2017] ICR 760 at [27]:

> …it is in practice hard to envisage circumstances where an employer who is held to have committed indirect disability discrimination will not also be committing discrimination arising out of disability, at least where the employer has, or ought to have, knowledge that the employee is disabled. Both require essentially the same proportionality analysis. Strictly, in the case of indirect discrimination it is the PCP which needs to be justified whereas in the case of discrimination arising out of disability it is the treatment, but in practice the treatment will flow from the application of the PCP. Accordingly, once the relevant disparate impact is established, both forms of discrimination are likely to stand or fall together. However, the converse is not true. If it is not possible to establish that the relevant PCP created a disparate impact, the case will not fall within the concept of indirect discrimination but it may nonetheless constitute discrimination arising out of disability.

*Summary: discrimination arising from disability*

Where menopause amounts to disability, s.15 Equality Act 2010 provides significant protection from treatment that is not direct discrimination. It is sufficiently wide to cover adverse treatment because of nearly all but tenuous effects of menopause, even where the employer does not know of the connection. Protection is not absolute though, and employers may be able to justify the treatment notwithstanding it being disability-related. In that regard, employers should generally consider reasonable adjustments before proceeding with unfavourable treatment, and the law of reasonable adjustments is considered below.

### Reasonable adjustments

The other part of the extended protection for disabled people is in the requirement for employers to make 'reasonable adjustments'. Where an employer recognises that a disabled person is at a disadvantage, it must attempt to remove it. It is not the case that an employer, in order to discriminate under this head, must overtly treat the disabled employee detrimentally; rather there is an additional requirement on an employer to spot a problem and remedy it.

That is going to be a relevant requirement in the case of someone disabled by menopause. Where an employer requires a certain level of performance or attendance, for example, but that slips in an individual case, that employer should consider whether its requirements need to be altered in order to level the playing field. It may be that that employee is female and of a particular age, in which case an employer might well wish to consider whether disability by reason of menopause is in play. If so, the employer needs to consider whether that employee needs assistance.

The duty to make reasonable adjustments is considered in detail below. It applies regardless of the type of disability so the duty is discussed in general terms albeit there will be no doubt that it would apply to an employee experiencing menopause (if that amounts to a disability).

s.20 Equality Act 2010 provides:

> (1) Where this Act imposes a duty to make reasonable adjustments on a person, this section, sections 21 and 22 and the applicable Schedule apply; and for those purposes, a person on whom the duty is imposed is referred to as A.
>
> (2) The duty comprises the following three requirements.

(3) The first requirement is a requirement, where a provision, criterion or practice of A's puts a disabled person at a substantial disadvantage in relation to a relevant matter in comparison with persons who are not disabled, to take such steps as it is reasonable to have to take to avoid the disadvantage.

(4) The second requirement is a requirement, where a physical feature puts a disabled person at a substantial disadvantage in relation to a relevant matter in comparison with persons who are not disabled, to take such steps as it is reasonable to have to take to avoid the disadvantage.

(5) The third requirement is a requirement, where a disabled person would, but for the provision of an auxiliary aid, be put at a substantial disadvantage in relation to a relevant matter in comparison with persons who are not disabled, to take such steps as it is reasonable to have to take to provide the auxiliary aid.

A duty to make reasonable adjustments applies to an employer (s.39(5) Equality Act 2010).

That duty is to comply with all three requirements (Sch.8 para. 2(1) Equality Act 2010).

The reference in s.20(3) Equality Act 2010 to a provision, criterion or practice is a reference to a provision, criterion or practice applied by or on behalf of the employer (Sch. 8 para. 2(2)(a) Equality Act 2010).

The reference in s.20(3-5) Equality Act 2010 to a disabled person is to either a person that has notified the employer that they may be an applicant for employment (for the purposes of decisions as to whom to offer employment), an applicant, or an employee of the employer (Sch. 8 para. 5(1) Equality Act 2010).

An employer is not subject to a duty to make reasonable adjustments if it does not know, and could not reasonably be expected to know, in the case of an applicant or potential applicant, that a person is or may be an applicant for the work in question. Similarly, an employer is not subject to a duty to make reasonable adjustments if it does not know, and could not reasonably be expected to know, in any case, that a person has a disability and is likely to be placed at the disadvantage referred to in the first, second or third requirement (Sch. 8 para. 20 Equality Act 2010).

s.21 Equality Act 2010 provides:

> (1) A failure to comply with the first, second or third requirement is a failure to comply with a duty to make reasonable adjustments.
>
> (2) A discriminates against a disabled person if A fails to comply with that duty in relation to that person.

*Provision, criterion, or practice*

Whilst there are three sets of circumstances in which the duty to make reasonable adjustments arises, the focus in this chapter will be on the first, the application of a provision, criterion, or practice ('PCP'). That is the most common trigger for the duty, and is likely to be the most common in menopause cases.

The discussion on PCPs under 'indirect discrimination' is all relevant and applicable here, and need not be repeated.

However, what is worth repeating is the importance of correctly identifying the PCP. With a reasonable adjustment claim, the PCP must place the individual at a substantial disadvantage when compared with non-disabled persons. That is a slightly different consideration from under s.19 Equality Act 2010, where the PCP must create a group disadvantage. The focus in identifying the PCP under s.20 Equality Act 2010 is therefore on the claimant and how s/he compares with people without a disability.

The formulation of the PCP must be precise, and setting out the nature of the disadvantage, which is not shared by non-disabled persons must also be precise. Otherwise, it is not going to be possible to understand what steps the employer should take to avoid that disadvantage, and the claim will likely be invalidated. That is highlighted no better than in *Crossland v. OCS Group Ltd.* [2014] EWCA Civ 576, where the claimant was a security guard, and was disabled by Type I Diabetes, which made him liable to suffer hypoglycaemic attacks without warning. The respondent supplied the claimant to British Airways Interior Engineering Ltd. ('BAIE'). He worked alone and at night. His duties included doing regular exterior patrols. BAIE asked OCS to replace the claimant with an alternative security guard, claiming that he had failed in several respects to abide by its working instructions i.e. exterior patrols. He claimed amongst other things, a failure to make reasonable adjustments. His case was that the relevant PCP was the requirement to carry out exterior patrols. He claimed that he was at increased risk of hypoglycaemic attack because of that PCP. However, he expressly stated that he was otherwise fit to work alone inside.

The tribunal found, which was upheld by the Court of Appeal, that the claimant's 'diabetic condition did not result in any increase of [the risk of an attack occurring] whilst working alone, and in particular did not prevent him from working alone in the office, there was no logical reason why he was at any different or greater risk whilst working outside the office on an external patrol. Therefore…the requirement of external patrols was not a PCP causing him substantial comparative disadvantage'. The Court of Appeal said at [40]:

> Mr Crossland's case was that, although a diabetic, he could, with one exception, do the lone security job as well as a non-disabled person and, subject to that one exception, he required no special adjustments to be made for him. The one exception was the making of external patrols. The reason, however, why that argument did not add up is because the *risk* of a hypoglycaemic episode occurring during a patrol was the same as the *risk* of one occurring in the office, yet the latter risk was not a disadvantage for which, as compared with a non-disabled person, Mr Crossland required any adjustment to be made; and he was, therefore, as regards office work, in the same position as a non-disabled person. In substance, therefore, the comparison [the tribunal] was making was that between Mr Crossland as a diabetic doing an external patrol and a non-disabled person whether doing such a patrol or

> working in the office; and that pointed to the suffering by Mr Crossland as a diabetic doing a patrol from no substantial comparative disadvantage.

The PCP must actually be 'applied', but that will likely be construed in the broader sense rather than by attempting to identify any particular point in time at which the employer specifically imposed any requirement on the employee (see *Rider v. Leeds City Council* UKEAT/0234/11 in which the respondent required the claimant to return to a particular place of work. Although that had not in fact been implemented, the EAT found that the requirement of itself could amount to a PCP). Further, nothing in s.20 Equality Act 2010 or Sch. 8 Equality Act 2010 requires the employer to have applied the PCP to the employee. It is sufficient that it is applied generally, and it places the employee at a substantial disadvantage when compared with non-disabled people.

In any menopause claim concerning reasonable adjustments, where it may not be immediately obvious what policy the employer applies that is having the adverse consequences, it is sensible to approach the identification of the PCP 'in reverse'; that is to say (1) to understand what it is that the employee is struggling to do i.e. the disadvantage and its nature, (2) why non-disabled persons are not at the same disadvantage (as a check that there is a comparative disadvantage rather than a shared one), and (3) what it is that the employer requires that has created that disadvantage. There is no escape from the fact that that requires a great deal of thought, and that it is insufficient to plead that 'the disciplinary policy' for example creates the disadvantage. It is also worth bearing in mind that the duty to make reasonable adjustments is not engaged in all cases in which an employee is disabled and disadvantaged. If it is not possible to precisely describe the PCP and comparative disadvantage, it may simply be that s.20 Equality Act 2010 has no application.

*Substantial disadvantage*

For the duty to make reasonable adjustments to arise, the PCP must create a substantial disadvantage for the employee, 'substantial' being more than minor or trivial.

The disadvantage must be one that is not caused to non-disabled persons. First, that means that the disability in question must cause the employee's disadvantage – see *Lalli v. Spirita Housing Ltd.* [2012] EWCA Civ 497, a non-employment case, in which Elias LJ, upholding the dismissal of the claim, pointed out at [47] that:

> ...the practice or policy which prevents the appellant from exercising the right of access to the community lounge is...the policy to bar from the lounge (at least at certain times of the day) those who are a nuisance and disturb the peace. The appellant does not contend that he could not stop himself from acting in the unacceptable way he did because of his disability; on the contrary, he simply denied that he had acted in that way...There is no condition of access which he, as a disabled person, cannot satisfy. There is simply the obligation to behave himself and act reasonably when in the lounge, and the fact that he did not do so had nothing to do with his disability.

Second, as above, it is not the case that a disabled employee that is subject to a disadvantage inevitably requires reasonable adjustments. Only where non-disabled persons are not subject to that disadvantage does the duty arise. The 'non-disabled persons' are a comparator group, rather than a single like-for-like comparator (*Fareham College Corporation v. Walters* [2009] IRLR 991). The purpose of the comparison test is simply to determine whether the PCP has the effect of producing the relevant disadvantage as between those who are and those who are not disabled, and whether what causes the disadvantage is the PCP, and the comparator group need not share materially the same circumstances (*Sheikholeslami v. University of Edinburgh* [2018] IRLR 1090 at [48]).

It is generally going to be simple in most cases to demonstrate the comparative disadvantage. Where an employer requires a certain level of performance, or attendance or punctuality, an employee suffering adverse effects of menopause will be able to establish that non-disabled persons are not at the same disadvantage in that they can, in general, meet those requirements of the employer. However, for example, a requirement to *increase* productivity may well, depending on the level required, affect all employees in the same way. Again, care must be taken in pleading such a claim to ensure that the comparative disadvantage does in fact exist.

*Knowledge*

As is set out in Sch. 8 para. 20 Equality Act 2010, the duty to make reasonable adjustments does not arise unless the employer knows of *both* the disability *and* the disadvantage.

Spelling that out, as it was put by the EAT in *Wilcox v. Birmingham Cab Services Ltd.* UKEAT/0293/10 at [37]:

> ...an employer is under no duty...unless he knows (actually or constructively) *both* (1) that the employee is disabled *and* (2) that he or she is disadvantaged by the disability in the way set out...As Lady Smith points out [in *Secretary of State for Work and Pensions v. Alam* [2010] IRLR 283), element (2) will not come into play if the employer does not know element (1).

The detail of knowledge and constructive knowledge is dealt with above, in the chapter on 'discrimination arising from disability'.

*Adjustments and reasonableness*

Once a comparative disadvantage is identified, an employer must take reasonable steps to avoid that disadvantage. It may be in some circumstances that there is no *reasonable* adjustment that can be made. However, the duty is on the employer, at all times, to investigate and make adjustments where reasonable to do so. There is no onus on the employee to suggest adjustments.

The duty, as set out in s.20 Equality Act 2010, is limited to 'taking steps' to avoid the disadvantage. It is not to remove the disadvantage. It can therefore be reasonable for an employer to have to make adjustments, even if the positive effect is only small. In *Leeds Teaching Hospitals NHS Trust v. Foster* UKEAT/0552/10, the EAT stated at [17] that it was sufficient for a proposed adjustment to have merely 'a' prospect of avoiding a disadvantage, rather than it requiring a 'good' or 'real' prospect, or that it definitely will remove the disadvantage.

Neither does the proposed adjustment need to, or need to have a chance to, completely remove the disadvantage. It is enough that it would reduce the disadvantage (*Noor v. Foreign & Commonwealth Office* [2011] ICR 695 at [33]: it is not correct that an adjustment is only reasonable if it would be completely effective).

The prospect and effectiveness are two factors in the holistic evaluation that the tribunal must make. However, where the prospect/effectiveness of the adjustment succeeding is small, that may mean that it is less likely to be reasonable (depending on the balance of other factors) when compared with an adjustment with high prospect of success/effectiveness.

Other factors in that holistic assessment are set out in the EHRC Code at [6.28]:

- The practicability of the step;
- The financial and other costs of making the adjustment and the extent of any disruption caused;
- The extent of the employer's financial or other resources;
- The availability to the employer of financial or other assistance to help make an adjustment (such as advice through Access to Work); and
- The type and size of the employer.

Of course, that list is not exhaustive.

It should also be remembered that an employer is not required to make the best or most reasonable of adjustments, nor the one preferred by the employee. As long as the particular adjustment made is reasonable, the employer will have fulfilled its duty (see *Linley v. HM Revenue & Customs* [2019] IRLR 604 at [38]). Whether reasonable steps have been taken is therefore objective, and an adjustment may meet the duty even where it is not acceptable to the employee (*Garrett v. Lidl Ltd.* UKEAT/0541/08). A step may be reasonable even if an employee had not asked for it (*Southampton City College v. Randall* [2006] IRLR 18).

One thing that is clear is that the reasonableness of adjustments is a focus on the practical result of the measures that can be taken, and is definitely not a focus on the process of reasoning by which an adjustment was considered (*Royal Bank of Scotland v. Ashton* [2011] ICR 632 at [24]). Therefore, a mere failure to consult in relation to the employee's substantial disadvantages and potential remedies does not amount to a failure to make reasonable adjustments (*Tarbuck v. Sainsburys Supermarkets Ltd.* [2006] IRLR 664). Of course, it may be that there were reasonable adjustments available that, through the lack of consultation, were missed, meaning that, objectively, there is a breach of the duty. To this end, the EHRC Code at [6.32] states that 'It is a good starting point for an employer to conduct a proper assessment, in consultation with the disabled person concerned, of what reasonable adjustments may be required'. Similarly, if adjustments are made that are objectively reasonable, there will be no breach of duty merely because the employer did not consult the employee prior to implementing them.

The number of potential adjustments is large. The EHRC Code at [6.33] provides a number of examples as follows:

- Making adjustments to premises;
- Providing information in accessible formats;
- Allocating some of the disabled person's duties to another person;
- Transferring the disabled worker to fill an existing vacancy;
- Altering the disabled worker's hours of working or training;
- Assigning the disabled worker to a different place of work or training or arranging home working;
- Allowing the disabled worker to be absent during working or training hours for rehabilitation, assessment or treatment;

- Giving, or arranging for, training or mentoring (whether for the disabled person or any other worker);
- Acquiring or modifying equipment;
- Modifying procedures for testing or assessment;
- Providing a reader or interpreter;
- Providing supervision or other support;
- Allowing a disabled worker to take a period of disability leave;
- Participating in supported employment schemes, such as Workstep;
- Employing a support worker to assist a disabled worker;
- Modifying disciplinary or grievance procedures for a disabled worker;
- Adjusting redundancy selection criteria for a disabled worker;
- Modifying performance-related pay arrangements for a disabled worker.

One issue that frequently arises in practice is that of an employee on long-term absence that states that it would be reasonable for the employer to continue to pay in full during that absence. One can see the attractiveness: the absence is no fault of the employee, and the policy to pay sick pay only for a specified period of time places them at a disadvantage. In particular, non-disabled employees are unlikely to be so affected given they stand more chance of not suffering long-term sickness. This could be particularly relevant in a menopause case. A non-disabled person is not going to experience the same effects and is not likely to be absent for a long period. Perhaps more relevantly the employee experiencing menopause is likely to be in a position to state that there is a prospect of a return to work at some point, unlike in other disability cases in which a return can be entirely unknown.

That concern has now largely been dealt with by the Court of Appeal in O'*Hanlon v. Revenue & Customs* [2007] ICR 1359. There, the tribunal found that it was not reasonable (under the Disability Discrimination Act 1995 albeit the principle must continue to apply) to pay full salary during what included disability-related absence. The EAT upheld that decision at [67]-[69] (emphases added):

> 67. <u>In our view, it will be a very rare case indeed where the adjustment said to be applicable here, that is merely giving higher sick pay than would be payable to a non-disabled person who in general does not suffer the same disability related absences, would be considered necessary as a reasonable adjustment</u>. We do not believe that the legislation has perceived this as an appropriate adjustment, although we do not rule out the possibility that it could be in exceptional circumstances. We say this for two reasons in particular.
>
> 68. First, the implications of this argument are that tribunals would have to usurp the management function of the employer, deciding whether employers were financially able to meet the costs of modifying their policies by making these enhanced payments...On what basis can the tribunal decide whether the claims of the disabled to receive more generous sick pay should override other demands on the business which are difficult to compare and which perforce the tribunal will know precious little about? The tribunals would be entering into a form of wage fixing for the disabled sick.
>
> 69. Second, as the tribunal pointed out, <u>the purpose of this legislation is to assist the disabled to obtain employment and to integrate them into the workforce</u>. All the examples given in section 18B(3) are of this nature...but none of them suggests that it will ever be necessary simply to put more money into the wage packet of the disabled. The Act is designed to recognise the dignity of the disabled and to require modifications which will enable them to play a full part in the world of work, important and laudable aims. <u>It is not to treat them as objects of charity which, as the</u>

> tribunal pointed out, may in fact sometimes and for some people tend to act as a positive disincentive to return to work.

Although the Court of Appeal did not deal with the general application of the point of full salary during disability-related absence directly, it saw 'much force' in what is said in the above paragraphs.

Note, however, in *Meikle v. Nottinghamshire County Council* [2005] ICR 1, it was a reasonable adjustment to pay full pay during sickness, but only where other reasonable adjustments had not been made in order for the claimant to return to work, which themselves resulted in the lengthening of the absence. The failure to pay full salary was not an independent failure.

It is also not always reasonable to ignore disability-related absences when considering sanctions under an absence management policy. In *Griffiths v. Department of Work and Pensions* [2017] ICR 760, the claimant was absent for 66 days, 62 of which were disability-related. She was given a written warning pursuant to the absence management policy. She claimed a failure to make reasonable adjustments in not disregarding the disability element of the absence. The tribunal did not find that to be reasonable in the circumstances. That was upheld by the Court of Appeal, whose judgment is also noteworthy for the following useful guidance at [80] when considering the applicability of s.20 Equality Act 2010 to potential claims (emphases added):

> ... In substance the complaint is that it was disproportionate to impose the disciplinary sanction given that the absence giving rise to it was disability-related. It is that treatment which lies at the heart of the complaint, not the failure to make an adjustment. The section 20 duty is normally relevant when looking into the future; it is designed to help prevent treatment which might give rise to a section 15 claim from arising. But that is not the purpose of the section 20 complaint here. It is really a staging post in challenging in order to invalidate the written warning — treatment which has already arisen. In my view there is a certain artificiality in arguing the case in that way. I respectfully agree with some observations of HH Judge Richardson in *General Dynamics Information Technology Ltd v Carranza* [2015] ICR 169 para. 34 when he said

that dismissal — and I would add any other disciplinary sanction — for poor attendance can be quite difficult to analyse in terms of the reasonable adjustments duty, and that:—

> 'Parties and employment tribunals should consider carefully whether the duty to make reasonable adjustments is really in play or whether the case is best considered and analysed under the new, robust, section 15.'

In other words, where a sanction is applied, the appropriate claim is not that it would have been a reasonable adjustment not to apply the sanction. However, if, say, the disciplinary procedure creates a disadvantage, which in turn leads to dismissal, it would be appropriate to complain about, not only the dismissal, but a failure to make adjustments in respect of the preceding process.

*Summary: reasonable adjustments*

It is tempting to assume that an employer must reduce any difficulty for disabled employees, or that anything regarded as adverse should be reversed or diminished. However, the legislation is far more exacting than that. The duty to make adjustments only arises if an employee can identify with specificity a PCP that creates a disadvantage, and does not create one for non-disabled persons. A great deal of thought must be given to crafting a claim of failure to make reasonable adjustments.

# CHAPTER SIX

# CONCLUSIONS ON DISCRIMINATION

The current law of discrimination does not neatly accommodate menopause. Disability discrimination is the most applicable form of protection, although it is not always the case that menopause will amount to disability. It is also not always the case that someone experiencing menopause will consider themselves 'disabled' and seek to take advantage of that protection. There is no doubt that the current law can be used in claims for compensation arising from adverse treatment related to menopause, but there are gaps and, until additional protection is created, some legal creativity will undoubtedly be required.

# CHAPTER SEVEN
# UNFAIR DISMISSAL

Employees experiencing menopause can face dismissal. If their condition impacts on their work or behaviour, their employer is likely to consider taking action. It may be that some employers will dismiss simply because their employee is experiencing menopause (albeit will offer some other reason as a cover). Those employees will have recourse under the unfair dismissal provisions in the Employment Rights Act 1996. As the following discussion shows, an employer seeking to act fairly will need to take into account, when considering any dismissal, the suggestion that menopause has impacted work. Failure to do so could mean that any dismissal is unfair.

s.98 Employment Rights Act 1996 provides:

> (1) In determining for the purposes of this Part whether the dismissal of an employee is fair or unfair, it is for the employer to show—
>
> > (a) the reason (or, if more than one, the principal reason) for the dismissal, and
> >
> > (b) that it is either a reason falling within subsection (2) or some other substantial reason of a kind such as to justify the dismissal of an employee holding the position which the employee held.
>
> (2) A reason falls within this subsection if it—
>
> > (a) relates to the capability or qualifications of the employee for performing work of the kind which he was employed by the employer to do,
> >
> > (b) relates to the conduct of the employee,
> >
> > (c) is that the employee was redundant, or

(d) is that the employee could not continue to work in the position which he held without contravention (either on his part or on that of his employer) of a duty or restriction imposed by or under an enactment.

(3) In subsection (2)(a)—

(a) "capability", in relation to an employee, means his capability assessed by reference to skill, aptitude, health or any other physical or mental quality, and

(b) "qualifications", in relation to an employee, means any degree, diploma or other academic, technical or professional qualification relevant to the position which he held.

(4) Where the employer has fulfilled the requirements of subsection (1), the determination of the question whether the dismissal is fair or unfair (having regard to the reason shown by the employer)—

(a) depends on whether in the circumstances (including the size and administrative resources of the employer's undertaking) the employer acted reasonably or unreasonably in treating it as a sufficient reason for dismissing the employee, and

(b) shall be determined in accordance with equity and the substantial merits of the case.

Reason for dismissal

Proving a fair reason for dismissal is a two-stage process: (1) proving the factual reason, and (2) demonstrating that it is 'potentially fair' i.e. falls within the categories in s.98(2) Employment Rights Act 1996 or is 'some other substantial reason'. Stage 1 is important. The reason for dismissal is not the simple heading 'conduct' or 'capability'. That is the category. The reason is 'a set of facts known to the employer, or it may be of beliefs held by him, which cause him to dismiss the employee' (*Abernethy v. Mott, Hay & Anderson* [1974] ICR 323). The reason is therefore, for example, 'the employee stole confidential data from the employer' or 'the employee was not considered competent for the role because they repeatedly missed sales targets'.

The tribunal must identify the real reason. It may be that an employee is dismissed simply because they were experiencing menopause. That would be unfair since it does not fall into *per se* the potentially fair categories. It is not likely that the employer would reveal that to be the real reason. In circumstances where there is a dispute over the real reason for dismissal, the burden of proof is on the employer to show their reason for dismissal. The onus then passes to the employee to show that there is a real issue as to whether that was the true reason. That can only be done by adducing evidence, and not by assertion alone. That is a light burden: not to prove the case, but to produce evidence that raises doubt about the employer's alleged reason. If that is satisfied, the onus is on the employer to prove its reason (see *Maund v. Penwith District Council* [1984] ICR 143).

## Fairness: generally

Where it is accepted that the reason for dismissal was an aspect of the employee's conduct or performance, albeit that stemmed from menopause, the reason for dismissal will not be in issue. However, the tribunal will assess the fairness of dismissal given the underlying medical reason said to be the cause of that reason.

Where capability (for either health or aptitude reasons) is in question, the simple test of fairness, incorporating both ss.(1) and (4) is:

> Whenever a man is dismissed for incapacity or incompetence it is sufficient that the employer honestly believes on reasonable grounds that the man is incapable or incompetent. It is not necessary for the employer to prove that he is in fact incapable or incompetent

(*Alidair Ltd. v. Taylor* [1978] ICR 445).

As was spelt out in the same case, that requires consideration of two questions:

- Whether the employers held the belief that the employee was not competent;
- Whether that belief was also reasonable.

Where conduct is concerned, the test is set out as follows:

> First of all, there must be established by the employer the fact of that belief; that the employer did believe it. Secondly, that the employer had in his mind reasonable grounds upon which to sustain that belief. And thirdly, we think, that the employer, at the stage at which he formed that belief on those grounds, at any rate at the final stage at which he formed that belief on those grounds, had carried out as much investigation into the matter as was reasonable in all the circumstances of the case.

(*British Home Stores Ltd. v. Burchell* [1980] ICR 303, confirmed as the correct approach to dismissals under the Employment Rights Act 1996 by *Foley v. Post Office* [2000] ICR 1283).

Broadly, those two tests are the same: genuine belief in capability/conduct; and a reasonable conclusion to that effect (which imports a reasonable investigation).

## Capability dismissals

In capability cases, there are steps to be taken by the employer that are typically expected by the tribunal, and the questions that the tribunal will ask will vary slightly between the types of case. Those types of case are: intermittent short-term absences; long-term absence; performance.

### *Short-term absence*

In intermittent short-term absence cases, the approach was summarised in *Lynock v. Cereal Packaging Ltd.* [1988] ICR 670:

> The approach of an employer in this situation is, in our view, one to be based on those three words which we used earlier in our judgment — sympathy, understanding and compassion. There is no principle that the mere fact that an employee is fit at the time of dismissal makes his dismissal unfair; one has to look at the whole history and the whole picture. Second, every case must depend upon its own facts, and provided that the approach is right, the factors which may prove important to an employer in reaching what must inevitably have been a difficult decision, include perhaps some of the following: the nature of the illness; the likelihood of it recurring or some other illness arising; the length of the various absences and the spaces of good health between them; the need of the employer for the work done by the particular employee; the impact of the absences on others who work with the employee; the adoption and the carrying out of the policy; the important emphasis on a personal assessment in the ultimate decision and of course, the extent to which the difficulty of the situation and the position of the employer has been made clear to the employee so that the employee realises that the point of no return, the moment when the decision was ultimately being made may be approaching.

It was also noted that medical evidence, in some cases, may not be required:

> Where one is dealing with intermittent periods of illness each of which is unconnected, it seems to us to be impossible to give a reasonable prognosis or projection of the possibility of what will happen in the future. Whilst an employer may make inquiries, it is in no way, in a situation such as the present, an obligation on the employer so to do because the results may produce nothing of assistance to him.

However, of course, if there is, or may be, an underlying condition that connects the absences, as there will be in a menopause case, the employer would be well-advised to seek a medical opinion.

*Long-term absence*

Long-term absences are different. There, the ultimate question is whether the employer can be expected to wait any longer for the employee to return (*Spencer v. Paragon Wallpapers Ltd.* [1977] ICR 301). How the employer reaches that conclusion depends on balancing all relevant factors. The tribunal in *BS v. Dundee City Council* [2014] SC 254 noted the following applied in that case:

> ...the respondents had a temporary labour agreement under which they could call on temporary staff to fill posts where required...The pay of such staff was the same as permanent staff...the [claimant] had exhausted his entitlement to sick pay and was no longer receiving salary...administrative costs and the costs of [occupational health] referrals...[the respondent] were a large organisation; it is obvious that such an organisation can absorb costs better than an employer with fewer employees. Against all of these considerations, however, it would be necessary to set the unsatisfactory situation of having an employee on very lengthy sick leave.

In *East Lindsey District Council v. Daubney* [1977] ICR 566, the EAT set down some procedural considerations in cases of long-term absences (emphasis added):

> Unless there are wholly exceptional circumstances, before an employee is dismissed on the ground of ill health it is necessary that he should be consulted and the matter discussed with him, and that in one way or another steps be taken by the employer to discover the true medical position. We do not propose to lay down detailed principles to be applied in such cases, for what will be necessary in one case may not be appropriate in another. But <u>if in every case employers take such steps as are sensible according to the circumstances to consult the employee and to discuss the matter with him, and to inform themselves upon the true medical position, it will be found in practice that all that is necessary has been done</u>. Discussions and consultation will often bring to light facts and circumstances of which the employers were unaware, and which will throw new light on the problem. Or the employee may

> wish to seek medical advice on his own account, which, brought to the notice of the employers' medical advisers, will cause them to change their opinion. There are many possibilities. Only one thing is certain, and that is that if the employee is not consulted, and given an opportunity to state his case, an injustice may be done.

*Performance*

Finally, in cases of under-performance, the NIRC considered the issues that arise in performance cases in *James v. Waltham Holy Cross Urban District Council* [1973] ICR 398 (emphasis added):

> If an employee is not measuring up to the job, it may be because he is not exercising himself sufficiently or it may be because he really lacks the capacity to do so. An employer should be very slow to dismiss upon the ground that the employee is incapable of performing the work which he is employed to do, without first <u>telling the employee of the respects in which he is failing to do his job adequately, warning him of the possibility or likelihood of dismissal on this ground, and giving him an opportunity of improving his performance</u>. But those employed in senior management may by the nature of their jobs be fully aware of what is required of them and fully capable of judging for themselves whether they are achieving that requirement. In such circumstances, the need for warning and an opportunity for improvement is much less apparent. Again, cases can arise in which the inadequacy of performance is so extreme that there must be an irredeemable incapability. In such circumstances, exceptional though they no doubt are, a warning and opportunity for improvement are of no benefit to the employee and may constitute an unfair burden on the business.

<u>Procedure</u>

None of the above 'tests' detract from the ultimate question, which is whether, irrespective of the matter in hand being capability or conduct, it was reasonable to dismiss the employee for the reason adopted. They are different ways of asking the same question: whether the employer gathered sufficient facts for it to be able to conclude that dismissal was appropriate. With any dismissal therefore, consideration of the investigation and the process by which the conclusion is reached is of high importance.

In addition to any procedural step set out above, employers are well-advised to follow the Acas Code of Practice on Disciplinary and Grievance Procedures (2015) and its accompanying guidance. Relevant principles are as follows:

- Carry out investigations without unreasonable delay [5];
- Where practicable, different people should carry out the investigation and disciplinary hearing [6];
- If it is decided that there is a disciplinary case to answer, the employee should be notified of this in writing, which should contain sufficient information about the alleged misconduct or poor performance and its possible consequences to enable the employee to prepare to answer the case at a disciplinary meeting. It would normally be appropriate to provide copies of any written evidence, which may include any witness statements, with the notification [9];
- Hold a meeting with the employee without unreasonable delay, whilst allowing the employee reasonable time to prepare their case [11];
- At the meeting, explain the complaint and go through the evidence that has been gathered, allow the employee to set out their case and answer any allegations [12];
- Allow the employee to be accompanied to the meeting [13-17];
- The employee should be informed of a decision to dismiss and the reasons for it as soon as possible [22];

- The employee should be provided an opportunity to appeal, which should be heard without unreasonable delay [26];

- The appeal should be dealt with, wherever possible, by a manager who has not previously been involved in the case [27];

- Allow the employee to be accompanied at an appeal hearing [28];

- Inform the employee of the outcome of the appeal hearing as soon as possible [29].

Whether an investigation, disciplinary process, and its subsequent conclusion is reasonable, is judged by the well-known 'band of reasonable responses' test, which is as follows:

(1) the starting point should always be the words of [s.98(4)] themselves;

(2) in applying the section an industrial tribunal must consider the reasonableness of the employer's conduct, not simply whether they (the members of the industrial tribunal) consider the dismissal to be fair;

(3) in judging the reasonableness of the employer's conduct an industrial tribunal must not substitute its decision as to what was the right course to adopt for that of the employer;

(4) in many, though not all, cases there is a band of reasonable responses to the employee's conduct within which one employer might reasonably take one view, another quite reasonably take another;

(5) the function of the industrial tribunal, as an industrial jury, is to determine whether in the particular circumstance of each case the decision to dismiss the employee fell within the band of reasonable responses which a reasonable employer might have adopted. If the dismissal falls within the band the

> dismissal is fair: if the dismissal falls outside the band it is unfair.

(*Iceland Frozen Foods Ltd. v. Jones* [1983] ICR 17, with *J Sainsbury plc v. Hitt* [2003] ICR 111 as authority for the application of the range of reasonable responses test to the investigation stage).

The level of investigation (including medical investigation) required is largely determined by the credibility of the facts presented during it, and it may not be necessary to investigate each of an employee's responses. In *Shrestha v. Genesis Housing Association Ltd.* [2015] IRLR 399, the claimant had over-claimed mileage expenses. He raised a number of explanations, in response to which the employer did not take steps to disprove. The EAT said of this approach, and of investigations generally at [23]-[29]:

> 23. ...The investigation should be looked at as a whole when assessing the question of reasonableness. As part of the process of investigation, the employer must of course consider any defences advanced by the employee, but whether and to what extent it is necessary to carry out specific inquiry into them in order to meet the Burchell test will depend on the circumstances as a whole. Moreover, in a case such as the present it is misleading to talk in terms of distinct lines of defence. The issue here was whether the appellant had over-claimed mileage expenses. His explanations as to why the mileage claims were as high as they were had to be assessed as an integral part of the determination of that issue. What mattered was the reasonableness of the overall investigation into the issue.
>
> ...
>
> 25. It is important to bear in mind the extent of investigation actually carried out. First, a comparison was made between the claimed mileages and the AA and RAC figures: it was found that the claimed mileages were *all* higher than those figures (in fact, almost twice as high). Secondly, a comparison was made between the claimed mileages and the claims for the same journeys in November and December 2010: it was found that the claimed

mileages were *all* higher than for the earlier journeys. Thirdly, the appellant was given a full opportunity to explain the apparent discrepancies, and consideration was given to all of the explanations put forward by him. The assessment made was that they did not provide a plausible reason why every single journey had a higher mileage. In my view that was a reasonable assessment in the circumstances and made it unnecessary to pursue any further inquiry into the explanations given. Nevertheless I consider below the arguments advanced on this appeal as to the specific further inquiries that should have been made.

26. The appellant's reliance on parking difficulties had two elements to it: first, that he sometimes had to park some way past the client's house because of increasing "residents only" parking restrictions and an increase of vehicles on the streets; secondly, that because the office had only a small car-park it was usually necessary to park on the street on his return, and the available spaces were some distance away....[The claimant's] argument in relation to parking was that if the employer doubted the explanation given, it should have investigated it by telephoning the local authority to ascertain whether new residents' parking bays had been installed, and/or by asking the appellant where he had parked on individual journeys and going out to check the position for themselves; and he submitted that it would have been very easy to check the position as regards parking around the office.

27. ...I do not accept that it was necessary in the circumstances to make such an inquiry for the purposes of a reasonable investigation. Nor do I think that it was reasonably necessary, or indeed realistic, to try to carry out some form of inquiry and verification exercise in relation to where the appellant claimed to have parked on individual journeys.

28. The other main point of explanation given by the appellant concerned road works...The only specific example given by the [claimant], in explaining why mileages were higher in June/July 2011 than in late 2010, was that there were road works 'around East Ham High St North'....he submitted that the employer could

> and should have asked the local highway authority whether there had been road works and what road closures there had been.
>
> 29. ...The tribunal did consider whether it was realistic to try to recreate the journeys, accepting that it was reasonable for the employer not to have undertaken that exercise. That was a conclusion the tribunal was plainly entitled to reach.

In the circumstances of that case, where the expected further investigation was extreme, and was to be into *prima facie* implausible explanations, it was reasonable for the employer not to carry it out. Each case will depend on its own facts.

It is unlikely to be the case that an employer would be entitled not to look into menopause as an explanation for performance, conduct, or attendance concerns. In any case involving an employee experiencing menopause, whose work is suffering as a result or who is alleged to have committed some misconduct where perhaps mood or judgment is impaired, an employer would be particularly unwise not to look into the matter.

Investigation into any underlying cause is better through occupational health or other medical advisor rather than attempting to base decisions on personal experience. That is what happened in *Merchant v. British Telecommunications plc* case number 1401305/2011. There, the claimant's performance suffered whilst she was under a final written warning. When she attended a meeting with the manager, who became the dismissing officer, she provided medical evidence (GP letter) that she was experiencing menopause. The dismissing officer had difficulties in assessing whether menopause was related to performance, but decided that he knew enough about the problems because his wife had been through menopause. Therefore, he did not investigate further. He dismissed the claimant on the grounds of unsatisfactory performance. The tribunal concluded that that was not based on reasonable grounds. That was because of the 'failure to have properly have investigated a highly relevant new feature that related to ill health that emerged for the first time at [his meeting with the claimant]'.

The tribunal stated that it would have been satisfied that dismissal was reasonable, and only the failure to investigate menopause rendered it unreasonable. That particularly highlights the importance of investigation into menopause and its effects when the subject arises. The tribunal described the manager as never being at the point of being able to reach a reasonable conclusion. That was because he was missing important information (if and to what extent menopause impacted on the claimant's performance, what the problems were, whether they were treatable, and a prognosis), and there was no reason he could not obtain it.

The tribunal described it as 'improper' that he relied on his personal experience of his wife's menopause. In fact, it went further in saying '...all women will experience their menopause in different ways and with differing symptoms and with degrees of symptoms...[the manager]...made a generalised assumption about how women experience the menopause and seems to have applied this to the claimant. He felt he needed to know no more. This would tend to suggest that he did not take menopause seriously'.

It is plain that, whatever the circumstance, whether illness, performance, or conduct, omitting serious consideration of menopause, whose effects can vary across all cases, creates a real risk of unfairly dismissing the employee in question. Seeking medical advice is a relatively simple step, especially balanced against the seriousness of the outcome to the employee. The tribunal in *Merchant* stands not to be the only one to believe that an employer did not take menopause seriously if it is not properly investigated, particularly where an employer would investigate other illnesses.

A further example of an employer disregarding menopause as an explanation for an employee's actions, in this case misconduct, is *Davies v. Scottish Courts and Tribunals Service*, case number 4104575/2017 (referred to in the chapter on discrimination arising from disability). The claimant, a court officer, suffered a range of adverse effects of menopause including stress, anxiety, and memory loss. She became concerned when she saw two men drinking water that had been on her desk in the court. Her concern was that she could not recall whether or not she had poured her medication into that water. She approached the men, who later reported that she had raised her voice, and informed them that her medication may be in the water. She was dismissed for, amongst other things, failing to manage her medication sufficiently so that she misled the individuals into believing they had ingested medication, and did so by shouting at them.

In forming the decision to dismiss, the respondent took into account its perception that the claimant had lied throughout the disciplinary process. She told the respondent that she could not remember if she had put the medication into the water, but the respondent did not accept that. The respondent was focused on the fact that the claimant had changed her position from initially being clear that medication was in the water, to accepting that it was not when an investigation showed that. The respondent gave no thought to her explanation for the change of position i.e. that she was confused and could not remember (an effect of her menopause). Instead, it believed that she knew that there was no medication in the water, lied that she thought there was, and changed her position once that lie was exposed. Having decided that the claimant had lied, the respondent only asked itself whether menopause could cause her to lie, which missed her point.

It appears that the respondent in this case attached almost no weight to the possibility of menopause-related confusion or memory loss. It is possibly unsurprising that the tribunal found the dismissal to be unfair, given that it appears that the respondent had closed its mind to anything other than the possibility of lying, and in particular to the possibility of the claimant's actions at all times being affected by her menopause.

Finally, in both these cases, and in all such cases, menopause will surely have a heavily mitigating effect, not least because evidence is likely to show that the behaviour complained of is out of character, and, if linked to menopause, is highly likely to be temporary. An employer realistically ignores menopause as a factor at their peril.

## Summary: unfair dismissal

It is clear that employees experiencing menopause are well-protected from a dismissal for reasons arising from their condition. That is not, however, an absolute protection, and in some cases an employer may well be justified in dismissing someone for conduct or performance concerns. Each case will depend on its facts, but what is accurate is that an employer cannot disregard the impact of menopause when considering their response to any problem to which menopause gives rise.

# CHAPTER EIGHT

# CONCLUSIONS: MENOPAUSE AND EMPLOYMENT LAW

At the time of writing, there are many discussions surrounding the recognition of the difficulties that menopause creates for employees in the workplace and surrounding the adequacy of legal protection. It is generally acknowledged that more should be done to protect those experiencing menopause, and this book has highlighted the availability (or unavailability) of protection, and the arguments that could be deployed to achieve (or overcome) it.

# MORE BOOKS BY
# LAW BRIEF PUBLISHING

A selection of our other titles available now:-

| |
|---|
| ‘A Practical Guide to Document Signing and Electronic Signatures for Conveyancers’ by Lorraine Richardson |
| ‘A Practical Guide to Transgender Law’ by Robin Moira White & Nicola Newbegin |
| ‘Artificial Intelligence – The Practical Legal Issues (2nd Edition)’ by John Buyers |
| ‘A Practical Guide to Challenging Sham Marriage Allegations in Immigration Law’ by Priya Solanki |
| ‘A Practical Guide to New Build Conveyancing’ by Paul Sams & Rebecca East |
| ‘A Practical Guide to Inherited Wealth on Divorce’ by Hayley Trim |
| ‘A Practical Guide to Shareholder Disputes in Family Businesses’ by Ed Weeks |
| ‘A Practical Guide to the Law of Forests in Scotland’ by Philip Buchan |
| ‘A Practical Guide to Health and Medical Cases in Immigration Law’ by Rebecca Chapman & Miranda Butler |
| ‘A Practical Guide to Bad Character Evidence for Criminal Practitioners by Aparna Rao |
| ‘A Practical Guide to Environmental Enforcement' by Christopher Badger & Stuart Jessop |
| ‘A Practical Guide to Hoarding and Mental Health for Housing Lawyers’ by Rachel Coyle |
| ‘A Practical Guide to Psychiatric Claims in Personal Injury – 2nd Edition’ by Liam Ryan |
| ‘Stephens on Contractual Indemnities’ by Richard Stephens |
| ‘A Practical Guide to the EU Succession Regulation’ by Richard Frimston |
| ‘A Practical Guide to Solicitor and Client Costs – 2nd Edition’ by Robin Dunne |
| ‘Constructive Dismissal – Practice Pointers and Principles’ by Benjimin Burgher |

'A Practical Guide to Religion and Belief Discrimination Claims in the Workplace' by Kashif Ali

'A Practical Guide to the Law of Medical Treatment Decisions' by Ben Troke

'Fundamental Dishonesty and QOCS in Personal Injury Proceedings: Law and Practice' by Jake Rowley

'A Practical Guide to the Law in Relation to School Exclusions' by Charlotte Hadfield & Alice de Coverley

'A Practical Guide to Divorce for the Silver Separators' by Karin Walker

'The Right to be Forgotten – The Law and Practical Issues' by Melissa Stock

'A Practical Guide to Planning Law and Rights of Way in National Parks, the Broads and AONBs' by James Maurici QC, James Neill et al

'A Practical Guide to Election Law' by Tom Tabori

'A Practical Guide to the Law in Relation to Surrogacy' by Andrew Powell

'A Practical Guide to Claims Arising from Fatal Accidents – 2nd Edition' by James Patience

'A Practical Guide to the Ownership of Employee Inventions – From Entitlement to Compensation' by James Tumbridge & Ashley Roughton

'A Practical Guide to Asbestos Claims' by Jonathan Owen & Gareth McAloon

'A Practical Guide to Stamp Duty Land Tax in England and Northern Ireland' by Suzanne O'Hara

'A Practical Guide to the Law of Farming Partnerships' by Philip Whitcomb

'Covid-19, Homeworking and the Law – The Essential Guide to Employment and GDPR Issues' by Forbes Solicitors

'Covid-19 and Criminal Law – The Essential Guide' by Ramya Nagesh

'Covid-19 and Family Law in England and Wales – The Essential Guide' by Safda Mahmood

'A Practical Guide to the Law of Unlawful Eviction and Harassment – 2nd Edition' by Stephanie Lovegrove

'Covid-19, Brexit and the Law of Commercial Leases – The Essential Guide' by Mark Shelton

'A Practical Guide to Costs in Personal Injury Claims – 2nd Edition' by Matthew Hoe

| |
|---|
| 'A Practical Guide to the General Data Protection Regulation (GDPR) – 2nd Edition' by Keith Markham |
| 'Ellis on Credit Hire – Sixth Edition' by Aidan Ellis & Tim Kevan |
| 'A Practical Guide to Working with Litigants in Person and McKenzie Friends in Family Cases' by Stuart Barlow |
| 'Protecting Unregistered Brands: A Practical Guide to the Law of Passing Off' by Lorna Brazell |
| 'A Practical Guide to Secondary Liability and Joint Enterprise Post-Jogee' by Joanne Cecil & James Mehigan |
| 'A Practical Guide to the Pre-Action RTA Claims Protocol for Personal Injury Lawyers' by Antonia Ford |
| 'A Practical Guide to Neighbour Disputes and the Law' by Alexander Walsh |
| 'A Practical Guide to Forfeiture of Leases' by Mark Shelton |
| 'A Practical Guide to Coercive Control for Legal Practitioners and Victims' by Rachel Horman |
| 'A Practical Guide to Rights Over Airspace and Subsoil' by Daniel Gatty |
| 'Tackling Disclosure in the Criminal Courts – A Practitioner's Guide' by Narita Bahra QC & Don Ramble |
| 'A Practical Guide to the Law of Driverless Cars – Second Edition' by Alex Glassbrook, Emma Northey & Scarlett Milligan |
| 'A Practical Guide to TOLATA Claims' by Greg Williams |
| 'A Practical Guide to Elderly Law – 2nd Edition' by Justin Patten |
| 'A Practical Guide to the Law of Prescription in Scotland' by Andrew Foyle |
| 'A Practical Guide to the Construction and Rectification of Wills and Trust Instruments' by Edward Hewitt |
| 'A Practical Guide to the Law of Bullying and Harassment in the Workplace' by Philip Hyland |
| 'How to Be a Freelance Solicitor: A Practical Guide to the SRA-Regulated Freelance Solicitor Model' by Paul Bennett |
| 'A Practical Guide to Prison Injury Claims' by Malcolm Johnson |
| 'A Practical Guide to the Small Claims Track - 2nd Edition' by Dominic Bright |
| 'A Practical Guide to Advising Clients at the Police Station' by Colin Stephen McKeown-Beaumont |

| |
|---|
| 'A Practical Guide to Antisocial Behaviour Injunctions' by Iain Wightwick |
| 'Practical Mediation: A Guide for Mediators, Advocates, Advisers, Lawyers, and Students in Civil, Commercial, Business, Property, Workplace, and Employment Cases' by Jonathan Dingle with John Sephton |
| 'The Mini-Pupillage Workbook' by David Boyle |
| 'A Practical Guide to Crofting Law' by Brian Inkster |
| 'A Practical Guide to Spousal Maintenance' by Liz Cowell |
| 'A Practical Guide to the Law of Domain Names and Cybersquatting' by Andrew Clemson |
| 'A Practical Guide to the Law of Gender Pay Gap Reporting' by Harini Iyengar |
| 'A Practical Guide to the Rights of Grandparents in Children Proceedings' by Stuart Barlow |
| 'NHS Whistleblowing and the Law' by Joseph England |
| 'Employment Law and the Gig Economy' by Nigel Mackay & Annie Powell |
| 'A Practical Guide to Noise Induced Hearing Loss (NIHL) Claims' by Andrew Mckie, Ian Skeate, Gareth McAloon |
| 'An Introduction to Beauty Negligence Claims – A Practical Guide for the Personal Injury Practitioner' by Greg Almond |
| 'Intercompany Agreements for Transfer Pricing Compliance' by Paul Sutton |
| 'Zen and the Art of Mediation' by Martin Plowman |
| 'A Practical Guide to the SRA Principles, Individual and Law Firm Codes of Conduct 2019 – What Every Law Firm Needs to Know' by Paul Bennett |
| 'A Practical Guide to Adoption for Family Lawyers' by Graham Pegg |
| 'A Practical Guide to Industrial Disease Claims' by Andrew Mckie & Ian Skeate |
| 'A Practical Guide to Redundancy' by Philip Hyland |
| 'A Practical Guide to Vicarious Liability' by Mariel Irvine |
| 'A Practical Guide to Applications for Landlord's Consent and Variation of Leases' by Mark Shelton |
| 'A Practical Guide to Relief from Sanctions Post-Mitchell and Denton' by Peter Causton |
| 'A Practical Guide to Equity Release for Advisors' by Paul Sams |
| 'A Practical Guide to Financial Services Claims' by Chris Hegarty |

| ‘The Law of Houses in Multiple Occupation: A Practical Guide to HMO Proceedings’ by Julian Hunt |
|---|
| ‘Occupiers, Highways and Defective Premises Claims: A Practical Guide Post-Jackson – 2nd Edition’ by Andrew Mckie |
| ‘A Practical Guide to Financial Ombudsman Service Claims’ by Adam Temple & Robert Scrivenor |
| 'A Practical Guide to Advising Schools on Employment Law' by Jonathan Holden |
| ‘A Practical Guide to Running Housing Disrepair and Cavity Wall Claims: 2nd Edition’ by Andrew Mckie & Ian Skeate |
| ‘A Practical Guide to Holiday Sickness Claims – 2nd Edition’ by Andrew Mckie & Ian Skeate |
| ‘Arguments and Tactics for Personal Injury and Clinical Negligence Claims’ by Dorian Williams |
| ‘A Practical Guide to Drone Law’ by Rufus Ballaster, Andrew Firman, Eleanor Clot |
| ‘A Practical Guide to Compliance for Personal Injury Firms Working With Claims Management Companies’ by Paul Bennett |
| ‘RTA Allegations of Fraud in a Post-Jackson Era: The Handbook – 2nd Edition’ by Andrew Mckie |
| ‘RTA Personal Injury Claims: A Practical Guide Post-Jackson’ by Andrew Mckie |
| ‘On Experts: CPR35 for Lawyers and Experts’ by David Boyle |
| ‘An Introduction to Personal Injury Law’ by David Boyle |
| ‘A Practical Guide to Subtle Brain Injury Claims’ by Pankaj Madan |

These books and more are available to order online direct from the publisher at www.lawbriefpublishing.com, where you can also read free sample chapters. For any queries, contact us on 0844 587 2383 or mail@lawbriefpublishing.com.

Our books are also usually in stock at www.amazon.co.uk with free next day delivery for Prime members, and at good legal bookshops such as Wildy & Sons.

We are regularly launching new books in our series of practical day-to-day practitioners' guides. Visit our website and join our free newsletter to be kept informed and to receive special offers, free chapters, etc.

You can also follow us on Twitter at www.twitter.com/lawbriefpub.

www.ingramcontent.com/pod-product-compliance
Lightning Source LLC
LaVergne TN
LVHW022100200926
848481LV00003B/1007
* 9 7 8 1 9 1 4 6 0 8 1 9 3 *